EXTREME
SPIRITUAL MAKEOVER

Developing Beauty
That Will Last

Kathy Fullerton

EXTREME SPIRITUAL MAKEOVER

Developing Beauty That Will Last

ESM PRESS

St. Louis, Missouri 63141

ESM PRESS

St. Louis, Missouri 63141

Extreme Spiritual Makeover

Copyright ©Kathryn K. Fullerton 2012

All Rights Reserved

No part of this publication may be reproduced, stored in a retrieval system, or transmitted in any form by any means, electronic, mechanical, photocopy, recording, or otherwise, without the prior written permission of the publisher, except for brief quotations in critical reviews or articles.

For information contact: http://www.kathyfullertonofficial.com

Library of Congress Control Number: 2012943457

ISBN: 978-0-9858055-0-0

All scripture quotations, unless otherwise indicated, are taken from the Holy Bible, New International Version®, NIV®. Copyright ©1973, 1978, 1984, 2011 by Biblica, Inc.™ Used by permission of Zondervan. All rights reserved worldwide. www.zondervan.com

Scripture quotations marked (NLT) are taken from the Holy Bible, New Living Translation, copyright © 1996, 2004, 2007 by Tyndale House Foundation. Used by permission of Tyndale House Publishers, Inc., Carol Stream, Illinois 60188. All rights reserved.

Scripture quotations from *THE MESSAGE*. Copyright © by Eugene H. Peterson 1993, 1994, 1995, 1996, 2000, 2001, 2002. Used by permission of NavPress Publishing Group.

Cover and interior book design by Sarah Fullerton

Printed in the United States of America

*This book is dedicated to
anyone who ever said,
"God, I just want to know you."*

*I want to thank my family and friends for
their love and support during the writing of this book.
Your prayers, editing, and patience were greatly
appreciated.*

Table of Contents

Introduction- Transformation is Possible   9
A Commitment to Change   15

What is True Beauty?   17
Day 1   Am I Beautiful? Defining Beauty On God's Terms   19
Day 2   Created To Be Beautiful   31

The Makeover Candidate   45
Day 3   Just One of the Family   47
Day 4   Say So   55
Day 5   It's Time to Change   65

Looking into the Mirror   75
Day 6   Into the Looking Glass   77
Day 7   Embracing Self Examination   89

Exfoliating Sin   97
Day 8   Rubbing Out Rubbish   99
Day 9   Liposuctioning Excess   109

Nutrition- Food for the Soul   121
Day 10   Tasting Truth   123
Day 11   Fuel to Fight   133

Water- Drinking in the Holy Spirit   151
Day 12 A Fluid Promise   153
Day 13 Liquid Power   161

Prayer- Getting your Daily Sunshine   175
Day 14 Walking On Sunshine   177
Day 15 Energy From Prayer   189

Exercise- Walking the Walk and Weight Lifting   201
Day 16 Doing Cardio God's Way   203
Day 17 Carrying the Burdens of Others   213
Day 18 It's A Marathon   223

Dressed for Success   231
Day 19 The Believer's Closet   233
Day 20 An Attitude of Gratitude   245
Day 21 Dressed for Battle   253

Budgeting for Beauty   261
Day 22 The Cost of Obedience   263
Day 23 The Cost of Suffering   271
Day 24 The Cost of Faith   281
Day 25 Becoming like Christ   291

Picture of Swan   297
Thirteen Week Study Schedule   299
Notes   301

Introduction

Transformation is Possible

Beauty is eternity gazing at itself in a mirror.

~Khalil Gibran

We are all familiar with the story of *The Ugly Duckling*. It begins on a lovely spring morning as a mother duck watches her nest of eggs hatch. To her surprise one of the little birds seems odd and out of place. Its big head and gray coloring does not match the brown and yellow downy feathers of her other delicate ducklings. The poor bird gets verbally and physically bullied by the animals on the farm, and decides to run away from the barnyard.

As the duckling sets off, it sees a flock of migrating swans. Something in its spirit relates to these birds, but it is too young to fly off with them and is left behind. As winter comes, the duckling spends the season lonely and miserable in a cave, hiding from everyone. When spring finally arrives, a flock of beautiful swans descends upon the lake in front of the cave. The ugly duckling has grown up and wants no more of the solitary life in the cave. With determination, the duckling decides to join the flock of swans, risking rejection once again.

To its amazement, the swans gladly welcome it into their group. The duckling is shocked when it sees its own reflection in the lake. It is then that the duckling discovers its *true* identity. It wasn't a duck, at all. It was a swan! The reason it had not fit in with the other ducklings and was considered ugly was that it was a different kind of creature altogether. The ugly duckling had been misjudged by others and had even misjudged itself. The world had applied the wrong standard in judging this creature and being misjudged had affected the swan's self esteem. Although initially unaware of it, the ugly duckling was *designed* by God to be so much more than a common duck, it was designed to be a beautiful swan.

Too often, you and I are like the ugly duckling. We live our lives feeling inadequate and ugly because we apply the wrong standard in judging ourselves. Just as the ugly duckling had been *designed* for beauty, we too have been designed by God to become so much more than we realize.

The Hope of Change

You may be living with low self-esteem because you don't understand that *you* are designed to become beautiful. **God's perspective is that you are an eternal being designed to be eternally beautiful like Him.** Developing your eternal beauty is what *Extreme Spiritual Makeover* is all about. This book's purpose is to help you:

- Understand God's purpose in creating you

- Give you a proper perspective on beauty
- Provide ways for you to start being intentional in developing your everlasting beauty
- And transform you from self-loathing sinner to confident child of God reflecting His beauty.

Expecting to Change

In his book, *The Life You Always Wanted*, John Ortberg says, "The primary goal of spiritual life is human transformation." Ortberg's words sum up why this Extreme Spiritual Makeover is worth your time. Just as a lowly caterpillar is created to undergo a metamorphosis in order to become an exquisite butterfly, you, too, are intended to *morph*. God actually created you to become more than you currently are. **God created you to be a magnificent specimen of beauty made in His image.** If you use this book with the expectation that *you will indeed change,* you will be on your way to becoming what God intended for you to be.

The Beauty Manual

Just as women refer to beauty magazines for tips on how to improve their physical appearance, we will be using a reference guide for how to become spiritually beautiful. During this makeover, the primary beauty manual will be the Bible. In order to become the beautiful person that you were meant to be, you need to understand God's story and what He planned for you as revealed in His Word. Becoming more beautiful in your inner person will mean knowing Jesus Christ and learning to become more like him. **It is through Christ's example that you are able to see what you were intended to be and what you will become with God's help.**

We will look to a number of stories from the Bible in order to learn how to become more beautiful. Over time, you'll find that your inner beauty directly correlates to your understanding of the Bible. The Bible says, *"All Scripture is God-breathed and useful for teaching, rebuking, correcting and training in righteousness, so that the man of God may be thoroughly equipped for every good work."* (1 Timothy 3:16) With this in mind, let's use the Bible to become more beautiful!

Taking Action to Change

Experts say that it takes approximately 21 days to form new habits. This book is to be read each day for a period of 25 days so that your old, self-condemning thoughts will be replaced with new thoughts that reflect God's truth about you.

Please stick to reading only one day's reading at a time. It will be tempting to move on to the next day, but you will get more out of this book if you will contemplate each day's message, talk it over with a friend or a group of friends, and implement the makeover tips. If you do this, your life will look dramatically different in just 25 days!

Each day's reading includes:

- **A Jewel of Transformation** – This is a kernel of truth designed to renew your mind about true beauty. Please spend time thinking about each day's jewel. By the end of 25 days, these jewels will form a beautiful crown of faith that will help you become all that you were meant to be.

- **A Verse to Claim** – Each day will include a verse from Scripture that you can commit to memory. This practice will insure that inner beauty becomes second nature to you.

- **A Question to Consider** – One major question will be given for you to think about each day. I encourage you to journal your answers to these questions in order to develop your personal code of beauty.

- **A Makeover Tip to Implement** – This is where the rubber meets the road. You will have an opportunity to take action steps to change your life. Becoming beautiful takes intention. Be intentional, starting today.

Some days, not all, have a section called "Be Intentional." This section gives you practical steps to change. You do not have to try to implement every suggested step before starting the next day, but you should pick one or two to try. Additionally, each day will end with questions for personal reflection or group study.

Why not commit to reading this book with a friend? Being accountable to another person is an important part of your makeover experience. It's time to commit yourself to 25 days to a more beautiful you. Let's get started!

Questions for Personal Reflection or Group Study

- How are you susceptible to applying the wrong standards to yourself when it comes to your personal beauty?

- This chapter talks about the purpose of this book. What are some of the ways this book is designed to help you?

- According to John Ortberg, *"The primary goal of spiritual life is human transformation."* What do you think this means?

- Why is the Bible a good beauty manual?

- What do you think this Extreme Spiritual Makeover will do for you?

A Commitment to Change

A Promise To Myself

I commit to spending the next 25 days discovering how to become truly beautiful with God's help.

My name

My friend's name

As iron sharpens iron,

so one man sharpens another.

Proverbs 27:17

What is True Beauty?

It was when I was happiest that I longed most... The sweetest thing in all my life has been the longing... to find the place where all the beauty came from.

~C. S. Lewis

Day 1
Am I Beautiful?
Defining Beauty on God's Terms

Charm is deceitful and beauty is fleeting;
But a woman who fears the Lord is to be praised.

Proverbs 31:30

A few years ago, I discovered a television show called *Extreme Makeover*. The premise of the show was to take women who were physically unattractive and transform them from ugly ducklings into beautiful swans, primarily through plastic surgery. I was immediately intrigued. Although this show appealed to my worst tendencies, I nevertheless found myself living vicariously through these women, wondering what my own makeover might produce.

The makeover began with a video biography of a woman describing the embarrassment and shame she felt because of her physical unattractiveness. Her problem areas were highlighted in a short segment. I felt sorry for the poor lady. Next, she went to the plastic surgeon's office to plan the makeover. As she shifted in her chair and bit her lip, it was obvious that although she lacked confidence, she was eager for change. Starting with her face, the doctor discussed the need for a brow-lift, a chin implant, and a nose job. He explained how he could refashion her face to make it more pleasing. The woman's eyes searched his for approval. After sensing his sincerity, she nodded in agreement as her comfort level began to rise. In my family room, from the safety of my couch, I wondered about my own face and what changes the doctor would suggest for me.

As the discussion turned to her body, the candidate confessed her frustrations. She was disproportionally heavy on the bottom and had the opposite problem up top. The doctor, of course, had solutions: liposuction, a tummy-tuck, and breast implants. The woman lit up as she picked "C" cup breast implants and viewed "before and after" pictures of liposuction patients. "I could use a little lipo, myself," I thought.

To complete the makeover plan, the candidate visited a cosmetic dentist to be fitted for veneers to give her a perfect Hollywood smile. You could see her excitement building as she saw that she would finally have a solution to her lifelong embarrassment over her crooked teeth. "A perfect smile makes all the difference," I nodded in agreement. Planning the makeover was already starting to give this ugly duckling more confidence. Personal nutritionists and fitness coaches consulted with her about proper eating and exercise to maintain her new figure after surgery. The woman did not flinch in the face of needing to change.

Now, it was time to implement the makeover. I watched with fascinated horror as the camera captured every nip, tuck, stitch, and staple. Some of the procedures were downright cringe-worthy. "I don't know if I could actually do that," I thought as I watched. Within a few weeks' time, the tens of thousands of dollars' worth of procedures had healed enough for the lucky candidate to begin her new diet and exercise regimen.

Finally, ten weeks after having been chosen, the makeover candidate was ready for her "reveal" in front of friends and family. As the proud candidate descended a staircase in dramatic fashion, the expressions on the faces of her audience were priceless. Like them, I was shocked at the change in her appearance. She really looked beautiful. She had gone from mousey to magnificent! I was happy for her. All the work and sacrifices really had changed her. The dream of becoming beautiful was now a reality. Everything was hunky dory, so why did I have this gnawing feeling deep in my soul that something was fundamentally *wrong* with this whole thing? I was happy, maybe I should say relieved, that this lady had been physically transformed because she really did have some physical flaws, but I was disturbed, too.

I think my conflicting feelings arose because the show promoted a perspective that I had tacitly accepted and yet despised for years; that a woman's worth is based solely on her looks, dismissing her character, personality, and talent. My reaction to the show made me realize how susceptible I was to defining my own self worth in this manner. Trying to be a Disney princess, a smokin' hot beauty queen, or a perfect Barbie doll leaves every one of us empty and depressed, and not just because we can't meet the physical expectations of others.

Focusing on physical beauty never completely fulfills us because we were created by God to develop the part of us that lives beyond our physical bodies. God's real purpose for you and me includes something much more than just the perfect Barbie doll body. **We are created by God to develop a kind of beauty that lasts forever in the part of us that lasts forever.** This beauty is not tied to what our bodies look like. It is tied to what our spirits and souls reflect.

Does this mean that we are never to focus on looking good? No. We are all drawn to physical beauty and want to be physically attractive. This is perfectly natural. The problem is that we tend to spend the majority of our time and energy focusing *only* on physical beauty. While this might be our natural tendency, focusing mainly on the physical aspects of ourselves causes us to miss a huge part of what being human is *really* about.

A Moving Target

> *The best color in the whole world is*
> *the one that looks good on you.*
> *~Coco Chanel*

Physical beauty is what most of us are chasing. One problem with ever attaining it is that **physical beauty is subjective.** If you are trying to gain acceptance by fitting in with what the culture is telling you is beautiful, then you are trying to hit a moving target because the perception of what is beautiful changes with the times. In the current culture, for example, tattoos seem to be all the rage. From actors and athletes, to the barista at Starbucks, everyone seems to be sporting ink. No problem. In order to fit in with the modern sensibilities, you go out and get a bunch of images inked into your skin. While they may be considered beautiful initially, there is a strong possibility that as time passes those same images will be considered ridiculous and dated.

The Greeks and Romans in ancient times elevated women who had full figures because those women symbolized fertility and prosperity in those cultures. Today, women of wealth in the Western world strive to be rail thin. What about hairstyles? Fashion magazines show short hairstyles one season and long extensions the next. The temptation is to spend our time and money on endless self-improvement. Just one more pair of heels that make my calves look shapely, another tube of lipstick that highlights the curve of my mouth, one more shot of botox to ease the lines around my eyes… blah, blah, blah. Chasing the moving target of physical beauty leads to feelings of inadequacy, not fulfillment. Women feel unhappy because they are applying the wrong standards to determine whether they are beautiful. Women are trying to find self worth and acceptance by chasing the moving target of physical beauty.

The Flower Fades

Even if you are fortunate enough to be blessed with the right features at the right time in your culture so that you are considered physically beautiful, it cannot be maintained forever because **physical beauty is temporary**. One thing that we must keep in mind is that our bodies are not designed to last. Go into your local nursing home. How many women in the nursing home have managed to avoid aging? None. Wake up and smell the coffee, ladies. Our hair is going to turn gray, our skin will wrinkle, our bones will shrink, and the physiques that we spend so many hours perfecting in the gym will waste away. Business experts tell us that women spend approximately eight billion dollars each year on beauty related products, yet the harsh reality is that no matter how many products we use, our bodies fade like the flowers of the field. Have you ever gotten a beautiful bouquet of flowers? They look fabulous initially, but no matter how often you change the water, eventually those flowers wilt and die. Sadly, you are forced to throw them away at some point. The same is true of our bodies. One day, we will all die, be buried, and eventually decay. All our efforts to be physically beautiful will, in the end, amount to nothing.

The Bible says, *"Charm is deceitful and beauty is fleeting, but a woman who fears the Lord is to be praised."* (Proverbs 31:30). How true this is! The word "fear" is referring to awe and reverence for God. We cannot make our physical beauty last, but our respect for God will last forever. When you have a proper love and reverence for the Lord, you have something worth admiring, something beautiful.

We need to keep our priorities straight, remembering that we will physically fade like flowers, no matter how hard we try to prevent it. Taking a more balanced approach, we should temper our efforts to keep our earthly bodies beautiful, while expanding our efforts to develop our eternal beauty.

Investing your time and effort to develop *this* kind of beauty is a wise use of your time. Spending twenty-five days in an Extreme Spiritual Makeover will produce change in your life, the kind of change that will put you on the path to true beauty that will last!

A New Definition of Beauty

So, how do we define this eternal beauty that God designed us to have? True, everlasting beauty is seen when God transforms your soul to reflect *His* eternal qualities. Fortunately, God gave us a human example of His beauty so that we would have a physical illustration of His qualities. His eternal qualities were perfectly reflected in Jesus Christ. Colossians 2:9 says, *"For in Christ lives all the fullness of God in a human body."* (NLT) **Your everlasting beauty will be seen as you begin to think and act like Jesus Christ.**

Thinking Beautifully

What we think in our minds affects, even determines, how we act in our bodies. **Your mind is the first stop on the transformation train.** If we are to define beauty as God does, we must realize that thinking God's thoughts is the key to being beautiful. Once we begin to think like Christ, we will begin to develop the eternal beauty we were created to have. Philippians 4:8 says, *" And now, dear brothers and sisters, one final thing. Fix your thoughts on what is true, and honorable, and right, and pure, and lovely, and admirable. Think about things that are excellent and worthy of praise."* (NLT)

Inner beauty is determined by *how* we think and *what* we think. Our thought life affects our actions. Your Extreme Spiritual Makeover is designed to help you begin the process of thinking beautifully, so that you will begin to act more like Christ. We will spend more time with this idea as we go through the makeover process.

Acting Beautifully

Once you begin to *think* beautifully, you will be-

gin to *act* beautifully. The Bible says, *"For as he thinks in his heart, so is he."* (Proverbs 23:7 KJV) Jesus gives us an example of a person's actions reflecting their inner beauty in the twenty-sixth chapter of Matthew. Jesus is in the home of a man named Simon shortly before he will be betrayed, tried, and crucified. When a woman pours some extremely expensive perfume on Jesus' head as a sign of her belief in his future sacrificial death and resurrection, his disciples chastise her for wasting expensive perfume on Jesus that could have been sold with the money then used to feed the poor. But Jesus knows the woman's thoughts and her motivation for anointing him. She has done this because she believes that he is the promised Messiah. Rather than rebuking her, Jesus praises her act, *"Why are you bothering this woman? She has done a beautiful thing to me. The poor you will always have with you, but you will not always have me. When she poured this perfume on my body, she did it to prepare me for burial. I tell you the truth, wherever this gospel is preached throughout the world, what she has done will also be told, in memory of her."* (Matthew 26:10-13)

Her faith-filled thoughts led to her righteous action. The woman's act was so beautiful, it has been recorded as part of the Gospel story that has gone throughout the world for over two thousand years. Acting as Christ would act is eternally beautiful.

Wouldn't you like to have beautiful attitudes and actions that define who you are and live on for eternity as a testimony of your inner beauty? *This* is beauty that does not fade.

As an Extreme Spiritual Makeover candidate, you must begin to approach beauty by looking at beauty from God's perspective. After all, God designed and created you, so it is only through thinking and acting like Him that you will find true happiness and fulfillment.

Questions for Personal Reflection or Group Study

- What standards do you apply to yourself to determine how beautiful you feel each day?

- What is one of the reasons we were we created by God according to Kathy in this chapter?

- Describe the two factors that determine if someone is eternally beautiful based on God's perspective on beauty.

- How beautiful is the part of you that will live forever based on the standards laid out by Jesus in today's reading?

Day One
Your Personal Makeover

A Jewel of Transformation: Eternal beauty is reflected in how you think and how you act, not in how you look.

A Verse to Claim: *"Charm is deceitful and beauty is fleeting; but a woman who fears the Lord is to be praised."* (Proverbs 31:30)

A Question to Ponder: If I could privately and honestly describe myself, would I say that I am beautiful? By what standards am I judging myself?

Makeover Tip to Implement: Take a favorite piece of jewelry and put it on knowing that it makes you look beautiful. Today, while wearing that jewelry, develop your internal beauty by thinking loving thoughts about some one in your life. Now, go tell that person that you love them! Remember each time you wear that jewelry to think loving thoughts about others and to say, "I love you," freely. In this way, you are thinking and acting like God would think and act. Expressing love is a beautiful thing to do. Record in your ESM Journal how you felt when you expressed love to another person. How did that person react?

Day 2
Created To Be Beautiful

Beauty itself is but the sensible image of the Infinite.

~Francis Bacon

When you witness an amazing sunset over the ocean or see an untouched blanket of snow on a neighbor's yard, do you sense that you are looking at something created by God? Oscar Wilde once said, "A work of art is the unique result of a unique temperament." I have good news for you…you are God's masterpiece! As His precious artwork, you were created as an expression of His personality. God wants to be known through what can be seen, heard, and touched in you. But God has an even greater purpose in creating you that is much more than skin deep. In order to understand *why* God made you, you need to understand *how* God designed you in the first place.

Made for God and Made to Last Forever

Steve Jobs, the co-founder of Apple, Inc., said this

about design, "Design is a funny word. Some people think design means how it looks. But of course, if you dig deeper, it's really *how* it works." **Design indicates purpose.** How you are designed is key to understanding how you are supposed to "work," or, in other words, the purpose for which you have been created. With this in mind, let's look at how God designed human beings.

God designed human beings with three parts – a spirit, a soul, and a body. 1 Thessalonians 5:23 says, *"May God himself, the God of peace, sanctify you through and through. May your whole spirit, soul, and body be kept blameless at the coming of our Lord Jesus Christ."* Each part is meant to relate to God and reflect His beauty, but each part plays a different role in that process.

First, Genesis 2:7 explains that God formed man's spirit as part of the initial creation of Adam, *"the Lord God formed man from the dust of the ground and breathed into his nostrils the breath of life, and the man became a living soul."* The term "breath of life" in this passage is the Hebrew word *neshemah*, which means spirit. Zechariah 12:1 says, *"The Lord, who stretches out the heavens, who lays the foundation of the earth, and who forms the spirit of man within him...."* **The spirit is the part of you that connects with God.** The spirit is the intuitive and conscious part that can understand an invisible God and worship His attributes, such as His holiness, goodness, love and mercy. This is why Jesus said, *"God is a spirit, and those who worship him must worship in spirit and truth."* (John 6:24) Your spirit is designed to discover, understand, and embrace God's Spirit. When *your* spirit is unified with God's Holy Spirit, you have the capacity to undergo the transformation discussed in this book. God made you with a spirit so that you would be able to relate to Him, know the truth about Him, and worship Him. Your spirit resides in your soul, so let's talk about the soul.

When God breathed the spirit into Adam's body, he became a soul. Look again at Genesis 2:7, *"The Lord God formed the man from the dust of the ground and breathed into his nostrils the breath of life,* **and the man became a living soul.***"* (emphasis added). This passage shows us that humans are their souls. C. S. Lewis once said, "You don't have a soul. You are a soul. You have a body." People often think that they have a soul, but this is not the correct way to think of it. Your soul is not something you possess, it is the essence of you, it is the real you. Your soul is your mind, intellect, will, and emotions. In other words, **your soul is your personality**. When the Bible says that your soul will live forever, it is saying your personality will live forever. Your body will die, but your essence, your personality, will live on. This is why your makeover transformation is so important. The Greek word for soul is *psyche*. It is from this Greek root that we get the English word *psychology*, which is the study of the mind and human behavior. When God transforms you, He is transforming your mind and behavior to reflect His personality.

The third part of being human is the body. The body is what interacts directly with the physical world. **God designed your body to house your spirit and soul.** It is important, useful, and beautiful, but like a bottle of expensive perfume, it's not the most important part of the product. The perfume bottle, although beautiful and useful, has little value without its contents. It is made for the express purpose of housing the perfume. The same is true of your body. Without the spirit and soul inside of it, the body is useless.

The problem is most of us are busy taking care of our bodies, while ignoring our spirits and souls. Turn on your television late at night and you'll see the cable channels filled with infomercials touting new exercise devices and diet plans designed to make your body look younger and more attractive. But focusing only on this part of you is a mistake. Why? **Because your current body is only temporary, but your spirit and soul are eternal.** Remember, your spirit connects you to God, and then your personality, or, if you prefer, your soul, conforms to God's personality in order to reflect His beauty and holiness. God wants you (your personality/soul) to be transformed while you are on earth. This is His great purpose for you. This is how you become eternally beautiful.

Not to say that your body is unimportant, but let's face it, your current body is going to die. After your physical death, your spirit and soul will eventually be given a new resurrected body in which to live. Your resurrected body will be the permanent home of your spirit and soul that will live with God forever, free from illness and death. This is a promise to those who love God and have faith in Christ. 1 Corinthians 15:51 says, *"Listen, I tell you a mystery: We will not all sleep, but we will all be changed, in a flash, in the twinkling of an eye, at the last trumpet. For the trumpet will sound, the dead will be raised imperishable, and the mortal with immortality, then the saying that is written will come true: 'Death has been swallowed up in victory.'"*

When God created us, He created creatures that He could relate to, love, and commune with forever. **God made us to become beautiful in the same way that *He* is beautiful.** This book is about how to develop the eternal beauty in your soul that reflects the image of God.

So what does it mean to reflect the image of God? What *is* the image of God? Let's talk about that.

Made in God's Image

The Bible tells us that in the beginning, Adam and Eve were made in the image of God. If we go back and read the creation story found in Genesis, we see that God made the heavens and the earth as a paradise. Within this paradise, the pinnacle of His creativity was mankind. Man was given the authority to rule over the earth.

> *Then God said, 'Let us make man in our image, in our likeness, and let them rule over the fish of the sea and the birds of the air, over the livestock, over all the earth, and over all the creatures that move along the ground. So God created man in his own image, in the image of God he created him; male and female he created them.* (Genesis 1:26-27)

So what does being made in God's image mean? **In part, it means is that Adam and Eve were designed to reflect God's nature, His disposition**. The translation of Genesis 1:26-27 from The Message gives a clearer description of what "being made in God's image" means.

> *God spoke: "Let us make human beings in our image, make them reflecting our nature so they can be responsible for the fish in the sea, the birds in the air, the cattle, and yes, earth itself, and every animal that moves on the face of the earth." God created human beings; he created them godlike, reflecting God's nature. He made them male and female.*

God expressed His vast creativity, complexity, holiness, wisdom, and beauty through human beings. Just as children reflect the physical, intellectual, and emotional traits of their parents and extended families, the first man and woman on earth reflected their Creator's image and qualities. They were without sin and perfect in their holiness. They lived in perfect harmony with God and His creation. **As God's children, Adam and Eve reflected His perfection and goodness because perfection and goodness are His personality traits.**

Henry Bullinger, the Swiss reformer, described it this way, "There was in our father Adam before his fall the very image and likeness of God; which image, as the apostles expound, was a conformity and participation in God's wisdom, justice, holiness, truth, integrity, innocence, immortality, and eternal felicity."

The Ugly Problem of Sin

With this creation story in mind, one must wonder what happened to the human race? If mankind is created in God's image, why aren't we reflecting His image by exhibiting holiness, truth, justice, wisdom, and integrity? Why do human beings mistreat each other, abuse animals, and pollute the earth? Why do we get sick and die?

The answer to these questions also lies in the creation story. The Bible tells us that God made one rule in paradise, *"You are free to eat from any tree in the garden; but you must not eat from the tree of the knowledge of good and evil, for when you eat of it you will surely die."* (Genesis 2:16) Perhaps this rule was a simple test given to mankind by God to see if they had obedient attitudes. It may have been a rule designed to protect mankind from evil. Regardless, the tree of the knowledge of good and evil became a temptation to Adam and Eve.

On Day One, we discussed how eternal beauty is tied to the way we think and act. Adam and Eve's perfect unity with God was tied to their desire to love and obey their Creator. Humility toward God in their thinking and obedience to God in their actions reflected God's image in them. But, there was a problem: Adam and Eve were susceptible to pride, and that pride led to disobedience.

When presented with the opportunity to be "like God, knowing good and evil," Adam and Eve fell to temptation and ate from the forbidden tree. Why would they disobey God? They apparently lacked faith in God. They did not trust in God's goodness. If they had trusted God, they would have believed that God's rule was for their benefit. Rick Warren says, "The foundation of spiritual maturity is an unshakable trust in the goodness of God."

In believing Satan's deception that God's rules were designed to keep them from being like Him, Adam and Eve showed that they did not trust their Creator. Remember that eternal beauty is tied to the way we think and the way we act. Their prideful thoughts, wanting to be like God and not trusting in His goodness, and their acts of disobedience, eating from the forbidden tree, broke their fellowship with God.

The Consequences of Sin

When Adam and Eve sinned, they lost the image of God. How? Three things happened when they ate from the forbidden tree. First, their spirits died. The Bible describes people as being "dead in their trespasses and sins," which is the condition of any person's spirit who has not had their spirit quickened and regenerated by God. All people since Adam and Eve are born into this world with their spirits deadened, which means that every person is muted in their ability to know and understand the truth about God, worship Him correctly, and fellowship with Him intimately because of sin. Some people say that we all have a God-shaped hole in our hearts. This spiritual vacuum is one result of man's spirit having died because they sinned. God warned Adam and Eve that they would die if they ate from the forbidden tree, and this warning became a reality when the first thing to die was the spirit. Thankfully, the Bible shows us that God provided a remedy to this problem through Jesus, *"But because of his great love for us, God, who is rich in mercy, made us alive with Christ even when we were dead in transgressions."* (Ephesians 2:4-5) This passage explains that it is God who makes our spirits alive, resulting in our ability to have faith in Christ (whether it is the Old Testament believers looking forward to Christ's birth or present day believers looking back to his death and resurrection), which makes it possible for us to connect with God and understand the truth about Him.

Second, when Adam and Eve sinned, their souls, which were made to reflect the personality of God, were corrupted and no longer reflected God's pure love and goodness. Every one born after the fall of Adam and Eve has been born with a sin nature. Romans 3:23 explains this, *"For all have sinned and fall short of the glory of God."* Remember that your soul is you! **The problem is that sin has corrupted you.** The crux of the Extreme Spiritual Makeover is that God intends to transform you back into His image. God wants you to once again reflect His pure love and goodness. Since you will live forever once you have trusted in Christ, your beauty will also last forever.

Finally, their bodies, which were designed to glorify God through obedience to Him, were condemned to physical deterioration and **death because of sin.** Romans 6:23 confirms, *"For the wages of sin is death."* This explains why our bodies deteriorate and die. God will raise up our old bodies from the grave, one day, and give us new, perfect bodies to house our transformed personalities. God intends to restore all things.

So, when Adam and Eve sinned the beautiful became ugly. The holy became common. When they sinned, God removed

Himself from them, because God's holiness cannot dwell with sin. The ugliness of sin robbed mankind of eternity with their beautiful Creator. The moment that Adam and Eve ate the forbidden fruit, the world changed.

The Journey to Restore Beauty

I plan on living forever. So far, so good.

~Anonymous

Thankfully, that is not the end of the story for mankind. Human beings lost the image of God in their lives and lost fellowship with their Creator in the Garden of Eden, but **the Bible is the story of how we can regain what was lost.** Many people believe that we are created in the image of God because of our creativity, inquisitiveness, and ability to apply what we learn to solve problems, but these qualities are found in all of the animal world and also in the spiritual realm of beings, including Satan, himself. To be creative and resourceful is *not* proof of having God's image. As stated before, God's image is tied to righteousness and holiness. These are qualities that *must be restored* in mankind in order for humans to be made in God's image once again. To reflect God's image in you is to have eternal beauty.

So how does God restore His image in you? God's plan is to put *His* Spirit into mankind to insure that eternal beauty is developed in His children, beginning with their redemption through the work of a Savior.

Yes, we are all broken people, whose lives are stained with the ugliness of sin, but through the redeeming work of God, we can be transformed from ugly ducklings in slavery to pride and rebellion to beautiful swans free the judgment of sin and free to experience God's love and grace.

Romans 5:17 says, *"For the sin of this one man, Adam, caused death to rule over many. But even greater is God's wonderful grace and his gift of righteousness, for all who receive it will live in triumph over sin and death through this one man, Jesus Christ."* (NLT)

The purpose of God all along was to not let the ugliness of sin that was brought into the world through Adam remain. The plan was to reveal the beauty of His character through Jesus Christ, who restores in us the beauty and image of God.

Jesus Christ gives us the Holy Spirit, who indwells us, enables us to live forever, and restores the image of God in us. Sinclair Ferguson states,

> God's ultimate purpose is to make us like Christ. His goal is the complete restoration of the image of God in his child! So great a work demands all the resources, which God finds throughout the universe, and he ransacks the possibilities of joys and sorrows to reproduce in us the character of Jesus.

God will use *all* of the circumstances in your life, the easy and the hard, the sweet and the sour, the joyful and the sorrowful, to mold you into the beautiful image of Jesus Christ.

This is the essence of your Extreme Spiritual Makeover.

Living in Truth

Your Extreme Spiritual Makeover is rooted in these truths:

- God created you to be beautiful in the same way that He is beautiful.
- God is in the business of restoring beauty by transforming you to be like Him.
- You are able to develop true, everlasting beauty because of what Jesus Christ has done for you.

Questions for Personal Reflection or Group Study

- What are the differences between your spirit, soul, and body?
- How does considering that you are designed to live forever and be with God change your perspective on life?
- As God's children, what did Adam and Eve reflect when they were first created?
- According to Henry Bullinger what does it mean to be created in the image of God?
- What happened to this image when mankind sinned in the Garden of Eden (look for three specific things in the chapter)?

- What is God's solution to this problem?
- How does this relate to your Extreme Spiritual Makeover?

Day Two
Your Personal Makeover

A Jewel of Transformation: You were created to reflect the very image of God.

A Verse to Claim: *"Then God said, 'Let Us make humans in our image, in our likeness...'" "So God created humans in his own image, in the image of God he created him; male and female he created them."* (Genesis 1:26-27)

A Question to Consider: How can I live to reflect the holiness and beauty of God today?

Makeover Tip to Implement: Take a picture of yourself and tape it into your ESM Journal. Underneath the picture write, " Made in the image of God to reflect His beautiful attitudes and actions." During this twenty-five day period, turn to this page each day and say, "I am made in the image of God and I will reflect His beauty in my attitudes and actions." Purpose to reflect the qualities of God in your life each day.

The Makeover Candidate

It may be hard for an egg to turn into a bird: it would be a jolly sight harder for it to learn to fly while remaining an egg. We are like eggs at present. And you cannot go on indefinitely being just an ordinary egg.

We must be hatched or go bad.

~C. S. Lewis

Day 3

Just One of the Family

We are family,

I got all my sisters with me.

We are family.

Come on everybody and sing

~Sister Sledge

There is nothing more exciting than bringing a new baby home to be part of your family. Whether through adoption or natural birth, parents anticipate what the child will look like and what his or her personality will be. When my husband and I were anticipating the births of our children, we wondered if our son would have dark hair like his mom and whether our daughter would have musical talent like her daddy. Regardless, we knew that as part of our family each child would be a reflection of us. This was one of the thrilling things about having children.

As part of your Extreme Spiritual Makeover, God begins by first making you His spiritual child. **The first step in**

restoring God's image in you is for you to being spiritually born and adopted into God's family. Once you are part of His family, you are able to begin to have the personality traits of your Father in heaven.

The Family Tree

The institution of the family was created by God to be the primary community for humans. In the family we are connected both genetically and relationally to one another. We find great comfort in relating to others who have similar physical, emotional, and intellectual traits. Who among us hasn't compared one family member to another member who has a similar trait? "Oh, she has Aunt Jenny's eyes!" It is easy to point to family members who have the comparable temperaments or talents. Our current families are but a shadow, or type, of what we will experience forever in the new heaven and the new earth with God, our heavenly Father. Our earthly families are a dress rehearsal for the actual performance. In this family we will no longer have dysfunction, but will rejoice in our unity and love.

God created us to become part of *His* family. Many people assume that every person on earth is automatically one of God's children, but Scripture teaches that we must be *adopted* into God's family after we become new creatures in Christ. Ephesians 1:4-5 says, *"Even before he made the world, God loved us and chose us in Christ to be holy and without fault in his eyes. God decided in advance to adopt us into his own family by bringing us to himself through Jesus Christ. This is what he wanted to do, and it gave him great pleasure."*

So how exactly do we become part of God's family?

You Must be Born Again

You became part of the human family by your first birth, but you become a member of God's family by your second birth.

~Pastor Rick Warren

In order to experience an Extreme Spiritual Makeover, you must be born again as a new creation in Christ. (2 Corinthians 5:17) Jesus introduced the concept of being born again when he spoke to a man named Nicodemus.

Nicodemus was a Pharisee, a religious teacher and leader over the Jewish people. His position made him an example of faith in his community. Having heard Jesus' preaching, Nicodemus wanted to ask Jesus how a person is able to inherit eternal life. Because of his position as a teacher, Nicodemus did not want the people to know that he had questions and doubts, so he decided to approach Jesus at night when no one else could see him. Jesus knew what was on Nicodemus' mind, so he cut right to the chase, *"I tell you the truth, no one can see the kingdom of God unless he is born again."* (John 3:3)

Nicodemus was baffled. How could an old man go back into his mother's womb? How could a grown person go back through the birth canal and be born again?

Jesus explained that the type of birth is like the movement of the wind. It is not something you can see, but just as the wind is real though you cannot see it, this spiritual birth is as real as a physical birth. This birth happens when a person believes that God sent His only Son into the world to save them from their sins. *"For God so loved the world that He gave His one and only Son, that whoever believes in him shall not perish, but have eternal life."* (John 3.16) This is where we get the term "born again Christian."

Remember that humans are created with a spirit, a soul, and a body. When Adam and Eve sinned in the Garden of Eden, the spirit of mankind died and all people who were born from then on, including you and me, are born with deadened spirits. This affects our ability to commune with God because God does not commune with sin. He is separate from evil. When a person is drawn by God to believe in Jesus, that person's spirit comes alive and is born again. This is what Jesus is explaining to Nicodemus. When you believe in Christ your sins are forgiven and you are considered holy and righteous because of Christ's sacrifice for your sins. As part of this birth into righteousness, God puts His Spirit in you, bringing your spirit to life. Like a breath or wind, God quickens your spirit.

When you are born again, you are considered righteous by God and you will begin to be transformed in your thoughts and actions to look like Jesus, your spiritual brother. Hebrews 2:10-13 explains,

> *God, for whom and through whom everything was made, chose to bring many children into glory. And it was only right that he should make Jesus, through his suffering, a perfect leader, fit to bring them into their salvation.*
>
> *So now Jesus and the ones he makes holy have the same Father. That is why Jesus is not ashamed to call them his brothers and sisters.*
>
> *For he said to God, "I will proclaim your name to my brothers and sisters. I will praise you among your assembled people." He also said, "I will put my trust in him," that is, "I and the children God has given me." (NLT)*

God chooses to bring many children into His family for His glory. Jesus' beauty, seen through his words and deeds, is the same beauty that we are designed to reflect as God's children. **The only way to start the process of becoming beautiful like Jesus is to be born again.**

Jesus went on to explain to Nicodemus that those who trust in God's Son will not be judged in the final day because they are forgiven. Jesus clarified that people who are born again do not have to stay in darkness because members of God's family are free from the guilt of things they have done in the past and can, instead, live openly and honestly in the light of day. Being forgiven makes it possible to reflect God's image in your life.

Do you have sins in your past for which you need to be forgiven? Can you see how God's forgiveness sets you on the path to being beautiful as He frees you from past sins?

By trusting that Jesus is God's Son, sent to die for your sins, you can be born again. The Bible says in Romans 10:9-10, *"If you confess with your mouth, 'Jesus is Lord,' and believe in your heart that God raised him from the dead, you will be saved. For it is with your heart that you believe and are justified, and it is with your mouth that you confess and are saved."*

The Benefits of Adoption

When you trust in Christ, God's Spirit will begin to change you. You will be adopted into God's family and receive the blessings of being a family member. **Being born again and adopted into God's family allows you to share one amazing benefit with your heavenly Father, the ability to live forever.** God's Spirit is the only thing that will never stop existing. God quickens your spirit, giving you the ability to discern the truth about Him. Then, when you accept Christ and acknowledge his sacrificial death for your sins, you are born again. At that moment God's Spirit comes to live inside of your spirit, guaranteeing that you will never stop existing. The Bible says, *"The Spirit is God's guarantee that he will give us the inheritance he promised and that he has purchased us to be his own people. He did this so we would praise and glorify him."* (Ephesians 1:14) (NLT)

It was God's purpose all along to spend eternity with His children. Giving you His Spirit is what enables you to do just that. **Your faith in God is your ticket to eternity**. But there are other benefits to becoming part of God's family. With Jesus as your brother and God as your heavenly Father, you are part of a new family that loves you and wants to identify with you. God protects, provides, and perfects you in the end. God wants to change you so that you reflect His beautiful image and look like a real family member! Your spiritual transformation confirms that you are His child. This makes your Extreme Spiritual Makeover all the more important.

Has your spirit been born again? If so, have you celebrated your adoption into God's family?

Questions for Personal Reflection or Group Study

- According to Kathy, what must happen at the beginning of the process before an Extreme Spiritual Makeover can begin?

- How do you become part of God's family according to Jesus?

- What are some of the benefits of being adopted into God's family?

- Have you ever been born again? Please explain.

Day Three
Your Personal Makeover

A Jewel of Transformation: The only way to start the process of becoming beautiful like Jesus is to first be born again.

A Verse to Claim: *"I assure you, unless you are born again, you can never see the Kingdom of God."* (John 3:3)

A Question to Ponder: Am I part of God's family?

Makeover Tip to Implement: In your ESM journal, create a spiritual timeline of important people and events that have drawn you into God's family. Is your spiritual birthday (the day you were born again) anywhere on the timeline?

Day 4

Say So

Has the Lord redeemed you? Then speak out!
Tell others he has redeemed you from your enemies.

~Psalm 107:2

Whenever you see a makeover on television, the climax of the process is the reveal. The reveal is the part of the show where the family and friends of the makeover candidate gather to see the results of the transformation. There is something deeply satisfying about someone being able to break through their old self and reveal a new and improved self. Having rid themselves of the things that dragged them down, they learn to soar. That is the kind of redemption and transformation we are all hoping for in our lives.

As part of your Extreme Spiritual Makeover, God expects you to have a reveal as part of your transformation. **The difference is that God wants you to reveal your change**

at the *beginning* of the process, rather than at the end. This may seem counterintuitive, but rest assured, God's plan makes perfect sense.

When I first became a Christian, I was told that I needed to immediately tell other people about my newfound faith in God and my commitment to Jesus Christ, but I felt uncomfortable doing this. I knew that I was a new creature in Christ and that I was supposed to look and act like Jesus, but I was just a baby in my faith. I wasn't able to act like Jesus in all circumstances. I was not particularly patient, kind, loving, or gentle with people. I did not exhibit self-control in many areas of my life. Quite frankly, I was no beacon of spirituality. There had not been sufficient transformation in my life for me to want to share my salvation with others. Inside my soul, I felt like an ugly duckling and a crawling caterpillar.

I wanted to wait until I was perfect to do my reveal. What I know now that I did not know then was that if I had to wait to share what God had done in saving me until my attitudes and actions were perfect, I would never be able to share that good news. I am never going to be perfect while in my earthly body. Being restored to God's image was going to be a process. My Extreme Spiritual Makeover was going to be a long and winding journey to beauty. Thankfully, God had a different perspective on how I look spiritually from the first minute that I was born again.

Positionally Perfect

So, why does God want us to reveal our faith in Christ at the beginning of our spiritual journey? Why can't we just wait until we are more beautiful inside? It is because when we accept Christ into our lives and are born into God's family, we have become "positionally perfect" in God's eyes. What does this mean? **It means that the moment you accepted Christ's death on the cross for your sins, you became perfect in God's eyes.** You were immediately forgiven for all of the things you have ever done wrong in the past and all the things you will do wrong in the future, and you are now in a position before your Holy Heavenly Father of being perfectly righteous. From this point forward, there is absolutely nothing more that you can do to make yourself more perfect in God's eyes. Jesus' death and resurrection put you in position to be called righteous. **If you believe in Jesus, you are ready for your reveal.**

The Bible says, *"Abraham **believed God** and it was credited to him as righteousness."* (Romans 4:3) (emphasis added). The book of Romans explains further,

> *'It was credited to him as righteousness.' The words, 'It was credited to him' were written not for him alone, but also for us, to whom God will credit righteousness - for us who believe in him who raised Jesus our Lord from the dead. He was delivered*

> *over to death for our sins and was raised to life for our justification.* (Romans 4:22-25)

In other words, **when God looks at you, He sees Christ's perfection, rather than your imperfection.**

You have become a family member accepted as part of God's family because of the sacrifice of Jesus Christ, and God's forgiveness has placed you in a position to be able to tell others of the righteousness that Jesus has given you.

The reveal is to show that God has transformed your eternal position upon your belief in His Son. Does this make sense to you? **It is not about what *you* have done to make yourself beautiful, it is about what *God* has done to put you in a position to be beautiful.** This is why the reveal in an Extreme Spiritual Makeover comes first.

It is key for an Extreme Spiritual Makeover candidate to reveal the transformation that began the minute she was born into God's family. Once you have been made positionally perfect by God, He begins the process of transforming your attitudes and actions to reflect His holiness and beauty. He begins to restore the image of God in you. This is a process of transformation that requires your participation.

A Birth Announcement

"Each time a child is born...the world lights up with

new possibilities." These words remind us of why God wants our reveal to come first. It's a birth announcement to the world. **It is our opportunity to shout out that personal transformation is possible.** You really can be a beautiful person who reflects the image of God in your life and lives forever in beauty and holiness.

Yesterday, we discussed being born into God's family. Today, we will look at examples of people who made their reveal to the world. This small act may seem inconsequential on the surface, but Jesus personally commanded that each believer take this step. The action of telling at least one person about the change that God has wrought in your life sets off a chain of spiritual reactions that have eternal consequences, some which you may see immediately, such as another person believing in God because of your testimony, and some which will remain unknown until you see God face to face.

Jesus set the first example of publicly announcing His role on earth when he was baptized in the Jordan River. In Luke 3:21-22, *"When all the people were being baptized, Jesus was baptized too. And as he was praying, heaven was opened and the Holy Spirit descended on him in bodily form like a dove. And a voice came from heaven: 'You are my Son in whom I am well pleased.'"*

Although Jesus' baptism was not a sign that he was being born again like an average Christian, Jesus was setting an example of using baptism as a public testimony. God takes this act of obedience by Christ as an opportunity to publicly announce to the world that Jesus is His one and only Son. This is an example to all who would follow Christ that they are to use their baptism to publicly confess their faith in Jesus, and confirm their acceptance into God's family.

After his resurrection, Jesus spoke again about public baptism. Jesus told his disciples, *"All authority in heaven and earth has been given to me. Therefore go and make disciples of all nations, baptizing them in the name of the Father and of the Son and of the Holy Spirit, and teaching them to obey everything I have commanded you."* (Matthew 28:18-20) This commandment encourages all believers to follow Jesus' example of being publicly baptized. It gives new believers a vehicle for announcing their spiritual births, highlighting their turning away from sin and turning to God in obedience.

An example of new believers being obedient to what Christ commanded about baptism is found in Acts chapter ten when Cornelius and his whole family are publicly baptized immediately after their conversions. *"Then Peter said, 'Can anyone keep these people from being baptized with water? They have received the Holy Spirit just as we have.' So he ordered that they be baptized in the name of Jesus Christ."* (Acts 10:46)

Say So

Baptism is a way to reveal your faith in Christ. It is to be done publicly and early in your spiritual life to show that Christ's death and resurrection make you positionally perfect before God. You don't need to wait until you have been transformed in your behavior. Baptism is a sign of the work that *Christ* has done, not the work that *you* have done. Use baptism as your spiritual birth announcement.

Testifying About Christ

A number of years ago, I was a discussion leader for a bible study that would take time once a month to let ladies to get up and share how they had come to know Christ personally, and how God was working in their lives. Based on Psalm 107:2, this event was called "Say So." The beauty of God was evident as the women recounted His faithfulness in mending their broken hearts, restoring severed relationships, and healing old wounds. As each lady stood and spoke, we all realized that God makes transformation possible.

Psalm 107:2 says, *"Has the Lord redeemed you? Then speak out! Tell others he has redeemed you from your enemies."* It is important to understand that God intends for His glory to be revealed through the redemption that Jesus provides. It is our job to be faithful to share that story. If God has saved you, you must *say so*. You must shout out your spiritual birth announcement. Baptism and public testimonies are ways to do this.

As an Extreme Spiritual Makeover candidate, you begin your journey by being born again into God's family through belief in Jesus Christ, and testifying to the change that God has brought about in your life. You must be able to identify Christ as your brother in God's family and you must be willing to share this good news publicly.

Just as the makeover candidate on television reveals her transformation, the Extreme Spiritual Makeover candidate must reveal that she has been born into God's family so she can begin her transformation to eternal beauty.

Application

The ultimate makeover begins when an unbeliever recognizes Jesus Christ as Lord and Savior of their life by asking him to come into their heart to be Lord. Ultimately, one must acknowledge the need to be saved from one's sins by the blood of Christ shed on the cross. You must accept His death as payment for the penalty of sin, and His resurrection as proof of the everlasting life to be shared with God.

Have you done this? If so, you are a new creature in Christ. *"Therefore if anyone is in Christ, he is a new creation; the old has gone, the new has come!"* (2 Corinthians 5:17) As a new creature, born of the Spirit, you are now able to develop the spiritual beauty that you were created to reflect. Now, it is time to say so!

Say So

Questions for Personal Reflection or Group Study

- Why was Kathy initially hesitant to reveal that she had become a Christian?

- What does it mean to be "positionally perfect" in God's eyes?

- When does God want you to "reveal" your faith in Christ?

- How is baptism like a birth announcement and what is it a sign of?

- How does testifying about faith in Christ help your eternal beauty?

- If you have been born again and adopted into God's family have you shared this good news with anyone through your baptism and personal testimony?

Day Four
Your Personal Makeover

A Jewel of Transformation: If you have been born into God's family, it is important for you to say so.

A Verse to Claim: *"Let the redeemed of the Lord say so."* (Psalm 107:2)

A Question to Ponder: Have I ever shared my faith journey with anyone? Have I been publicly baptized?

Makeover Tip to Implement: Take the spiritual timeline that you created yesterday and share it with one person.

Day 5
It's Time to Change

Amazing Grace, how sweet the sound,

That saved a wretch like me...

I once was lost but now am found,

was blind, but now, I see.

~John Newton

Any good makeover starts with the idea that the person being transformed actually *wants* to change. **Today, as you continue on your Extreme Spiritual Makeover, you must realize that God will change you and develop your inner beauty only as you reveal to Him *your* desire to change.** Because God wants a relationship with you, He provides life circumstances unique to you that are designed to draw you to Him. Some people turn to God easily and seem eager to make changes in their lives, while others resist change at all cost. But even if you are as stubborn as a mule, because of His great love for you, God will pursue you, even though you may be running from change or fighting the need to change. God will put in your path whatever you may need to cause you to realize that you need Him in order to fill the God-shaped hole in your soul. This is what happened to a man named John Newton.

Time for Change

In 1725, John Newton was born in London, England to a shipmaster in the royal navy. By the time he was eleven years old, his mother had died, so John went to sea with his father, spending six years sailing until his father decided to retire from life on the sea. Although his father was done with the sea, John was just beginning a stormy life of sailing and adventure. John was always getting into conflicts with other people and his bad temper eventually got him kicked off a slave trading ship and given to an African duchess to be her slave. Now, instead of trading slaves, John had become a slave, himself.

He languished in Africa for a number of years until his father discovered his whereabouts and sent a sea captain to rescue him. On the voyage home to England, his ship ran into a terrible storm that threatened to sink the ship and take the life of every man on board. This was the last straw for John. Having lost his mother at an early age, been kicked off of a ship because of his temper, endured the humiliation of slavery, and now facing death because of a storm, He finally hit bottom and cried out to God for salvation as the ship filled with water. By God's providence, the hole in the ship's hull, which was causing the ship to sink, was stopped up by cargo, and the ship eventually made it safely to shore. John, however, spent the rest of the voyage home reading the Bible in search of God.

John Newton was ready for change. God used the circumstances in his life to humble him and cause him to be ready for change. His conversion to Christ began a lifelong spiritual transformation that eventually led John to become a priest in the Church of England, where he composed hundreds of hymns to accompany his sermons, including the famous hymn *Amazing Grace*. John's change meant that instead of being part of the horrible slave trade that enslaved countless souls, he became a man who helped people throw off the chains of slavery to sin by finding freedom in Christ. John became a change agent for others because his life began to reflect God's holiness and love for people. This man had an Extreme Spiritual Makeover!

How might God use circumstances in your life to draw you to Him? Do you see these hardships as opportunities to become more eternally beautiful?

Wrestling with God

Sometimes we fight against change. Do you *want* to change or are you wrestling *against* change? Perhaps you have a personality problem like John Newton that is keeping you from starting your spiritual makeover. God can triumph over your resistance to change. He loves you so much that He is willing to fight for your transformation. Because you are his precious child, God wants the best for you, and He will fashion a scenario in your life that will break you, if that is what it takes to humble you. If God takes this approach with you, it can feel like you are in the greatest wrestling match of your life, but you can rest in the knowledge that God *is* going to win and when God has a victory over you, it is truly a win-win situation. This is what happened to a man named Jacob, who fought against God until he could fight no more. At the end of his rope, he finally asked God for His blessing.

In Genesis 32 we find the story of Jacob, whose name means "holder of the heel" or "supplanter." It was an appropriate name because Jacob was a crafty man who managed to trick his older twin brother out of his family blessing and inheritance as the oldest son. For Jacob, these were a means for him to inherit God's promise to bless this particular family and the world by sending the Savior through Abraham's (Jacob's grandfather) lineage and to give this family the Promised Land as an eternal inheritance. This was a very big deal and Jacob was underhanded in manipulating the situation. Although Jacob started out as a rascal, God used circumstances in Jacob's life to humble him because He wanted to transform Jacob, in addition to giving him the promised blessing and inheritance.

The circumstances that would humble him started after Jacob duped his father and brother out of the blessing and inheritance, fled his home, and went to a distant land where

It's Time to Change

he endured trials under his Uncle Laban. Even though Laban was unfair to him, Jacob persisted, eventually gaining wealth and a large family. The situation with Laban was very difficult though, and God used this as an opportunity to put Jacob between a rock and a hard place. By commanding Jacob to go back to his homeland and his twin brother, God was fashioning a breaking point to bring Jacob to the brink of change.

Contemplating that he and his family might die at the hands of his angry twin brother, Jacob started the night in prayer and ended up wrestling with God. The Bible describes a man coming to wrestle with Jacob. Who is this man? The book of Hosea gives commentary on this incident, speaking of Jacob,

> *In the womb he grasped his brother's heel: as a man he struggled with God. He struggled with the angel and overcame him; he wept and begged for his favor. He found him at Bethel and talked with him there– the Lord God Almighty, the Lord is his name of renown!* (Hosea 12:3-5)

The Bible explains that Jacob was very strong-willed and wrestled with God, but ended up asking God for His favor and blessing.

Have you ever experienced this? You go to God to pray about something, but the reality is that you want God to give you what *you* want on *your* terms. This is how Jacob had approached his whole spiritual life. He had tricked everyone to get God's blessing, he tricked his father-in-law to get wealthy, and now, he wanted God to bless him once again, without ever having to change anything about his personality or sinfulness. But God wanted more for Jacob. God wanted to bless Jacob by changing his heart and transforming him from being prideful to being humble. It was a mighty struggle and Jacob was not easily subdued. God actually wrenched Jacob's hip in order to weaken him. Finally, Jacob was no longer fighting with God so much as he was hanging onto God. In this weakened state Jacob cried out, "*I will not let you go unless you bless me.*" (Genesis 32:26) Staying true to his tenacious and persistent personality, Jacob came to a point in his life where he wanted to change. He was ready to surrender to God's will and give up his own will.

From that point on, Jacob was transformed. God changed his name to Israel, which means, "has wrestled with man and God, and has overcome." Thereafter, his life exhibited humility, beauty, and grace. Finally, Jacob began to reflect the beautiful image of God in his life. He had known God before this incident, but had never really allowed God to change his personality. After this night of wrestling with God, Jacob really wanted to change. God responded to Jacob's desire and he experienced an Extreme Spiritual Makeover.

Are you fighting with God against change and transformation

in your life? Has God brought you to the brink of change through hard circumstances? Why not listen to God and humbly ask for His blessing? Once you do this, you will experience what God can do when you really *want* to change.

Wanting to Change

There is no better example of someone wanting to transform herself than a bride-to-be. I can remember spending the whole year before my wedding dieting and exercising to make sure that I would look my best when I walked down that aisle. My desire to look good for my groom and my family and friends made the work of transformation effortless. I had the proper perspective to do the work necessary to achieve my goals because I was motivated to change.

The Bible describes the Church as Christ's Bride. *"For the wedding of the Lamb has come, and His Bride has made herself ready. Fine linen, bright and clean was given her to wear. (Fine linen stands for the righteous acts of the saints)."* (Revelation 19:7-8) Just as brides-to-be are motivated to be outwardly beautiful for their groom, you should be equally motivated to be inwardly beautiful for Christ. As your love for God grows, God's Spirit will work in and through your personality to change you from the inside. God responds to your love by putting His Holy Spirit inside of you and transforming you.

Once you are born into God's family and have made a public statement of your faith, God begins a relationship with you that includes His Holy Spirit watching and responding to you as you indicate your desire to be more like Christ.

Questions for Personal Reflection or Group Study

- How have you wrestled against change like Jacob?

- How has God wrenched you until you were ready to humble yourself and change?

- If God did not bring trials to cause your change, what served as your motivation to change?

- How would you explain to a friend how the desire to change makes all the difference in the process?

Day Five

Your Personal Makeover

Jewel of Transformation: Transformation begins when you actually *want* to change.

A Verse to Claim: *"I will not let you go unless you bless me."* (Genesis 32:26)

A Question to Ponder: Am I ready to make changes in my life and will I cling to God to receive His blessings in my life?

Makeover Tip to Implement: Spend some time alone thinking about those things with which you wrestle in life. Make an honest list. Light a candle and write a personal prayer to God in your ESM journal, asking God for the strength to deal with these issues. Ask for God to bless you in your struggles. Write in your journal what you are willing to change about yourself.

Looking Into the Mirror

There are times when we should be content
with what we have,
but never content with what we are.
~William George Jordan

Day 6
Into the Looking Glass

For the word of God is alive and active.

Sharper than any double-edged sword,

it penetrates even to dividing the soul and

Spirit, joints and marrow; it judges the

thoughts and attitudes of the heart.

~Hebrews 4:12

Each morning, one of the first things we do when we get out of bed is to look at ourselves in the mirror. When you think about it, it is really a curious thing to do because it is doubtful that any of us look our best at that point. So why do we consistently do it? There seems to be something within us that compels us to take an inventory of our physical appearance. Perhaps our subconscious is thinking, "Yep. I'm still here and I'm still me." Throughout the day, we look into the mirror to make sure that our hair is in place, our make-up isn't smudged, and our clothes are hanging properly. There is comfort and confirmation in the mirror because in the mirror we see ourselves as we really are. If we need fixing, the mirror guides us to what needs change.

As Extreme Spiritual Makeover candidates, we need to look into a different kind of mirror each day to check how we look spiritually. This spiritual mirror shows us how our personalities compare to Christ's personality. Rather than checking to see if we have unsightly blemishes, tangled hair, or swollen, puffy eyes, we must look into our souls to see if we have bad attitudes, tangled relationships, and swollen pride. Do we have glaring flaws? What will the mirror into our souls reveal?

Finding a Trusty Reflection

The first order of business is to find a trusty mirror. There is nothing worse than an inaccurate mirror. Department stores are filled with these. Perhaps this has happened to you. You decide to go bathing suit shopping at the mall. (That was your first mistake.) You find a cute suit in your size and go into the dressing room to try it on. That is when you realize that the department store mirror makes you look fifteen pounds heavier. Surely the image that is being reflected back to you is incorrect. It doesn't help that florescent lights make you look like you died two years ago. The mirror is "off." This is very similar to what happens to us if we make the mistake of relying on societal norms and the media to define what is beautiful. We might as well be looking into a fun house mirror under florescent lights.

So what kind of "mirror" can we use to accurately see what is invisible, the condition of our souls? **The Bible is our spiritual mirror.** It is trustworthy and accurate. In order for us to determine how we look according to God's standards of beauty, we must look to Scripture. Rather than just judging yourself physically each day, the Extreme Spiritual Makeover candidate should look to the Bible to gauge how her eternal beauty is developing. The Bible says, *"For the word of God is alive and active. Sharper than any double-edged sword, it penetrates even to dividing the soul and spirit, joints and marrow; it judges the thoughts and attitudes of the heart."* (Hebrews 4:12) Now, *that* is a mirror! Scripture is alive, penetrating your soul and spirit, and making clear the appearance of your thoughts and attitudes. In Scripture, we are able to see the true nature of our souls. If we want to know whether we are beautiful according to God's standard, we need only to look at Scripture.

The Bible is the mirror that shows us the ugliness inside of ourselves. Just as we may look into a physical mirror and see that we have a blemish on our face that needs acne cream to heal, we look into the spiritual mirror of the Bible to see what blemishes are in our souls that need transformation. This is an important part of the process of restoring God's beauty in us. Once you see the ugliness that comes from your sinful nature, as compared to the beauty of God's holiness, you can confess the flaws you see to God. Once you have confessed, God responds to your humble heart and transforms you into a person who thinks and behaves in beautiful ways that please Him and reflect His beauty. Humility is the key to admitting ugliness in the soul. But first, we have to be able to see what God considers ugly.

The Law - Behaviors Matter

The Ten Commandments are like a mirror for your soul. Long ago, God made a man named Moses the leader of the people descended from Israel (Jacob). Moses was an amazing man. He was chosen by God to be a prophet to the Pharaoh in Egypt and to lead the Israelites out of slavery and into the Promised Land. Additionally, God gave Moses His Law for all mankind. The Ten Commandments served as part of the greater moral guide, as well as the civil and criminal legal system for the Israelites. It eventually formed the basis for the civil and criminal law of the Western world, too. What many people do not realize is *why* God gave us the Ten Commandments. They are a set of behavioral standards given to help people see how they measure up to God's standard of holiness and perfection. Are you familiar with the Ten Commandments? Could you recite them right now from memory? Here is God's holy standard of beautiful behavior as found in Exodus 20:1-17:

The Ten Commandments

1. You shall have no other gods before me.

2. You shall not make for yourself any idol in the form of anything in heaven or on the earth or in the water below: You shall not bow down to worship them, nor serve them.

3. You shall not misuse the name of the LORD your God, for the LORD will not hold anyone guiltless who misuses his name.

4. Remember the Sabbath day by keeping it holy. Six days you shall labor, and do all your work, but the seventh day is the Sabbath to the LORD your God: On it you shall not do any work, neither your son or daughter, nor your manservant or maidservant, nor your animals, nor the foreigner within your gates: For in six days the LORD made the heavens and the earth, the sea, and all that in them is, but he rested on the seventh day: Therefore the LORD blessed the Sabbath day, and made it holy.

5. Honor your father and mother, so that you may live long upon in the land the LORD God is giving you.

6. You shall not murder.

7. You shall not commit adultery.

8. You shall not steal.

9. You shall not bear false testimony against your neighbor.

10. You shall not covet your neighbor's house, you shall not covet your neighbor's wife, or his manservant, or his maidservant, his ox, donkey, or anything that belongs to your neighbor.

The first four commandments show how people should relate to God. The last six commandments define how people should relate to other people. It is clear that we are commanded by God to behave so that we honor God and love other people. In a perfect world, we would never do anything to slight the holiness of God or harm another person.

There is no doubt that this is an impossible standard to live up to. Why? Because when Adam and Eve fell in the Garden of Eden, all of their subsequent descendants, including you and me, inherited a sinful nature from them. It is against our nature to be able to perfectly fulfill God's Ten Commandments. Regardless, this Law is a mirror for your soul. How do you look in this mirror?

The Beatitudes - Attitudes Matter

When Jesus came to earth, he, too, had something to say about how our lives should look. In the book of Matthew, Jesus gives the Sermon on the Mount. Unlike the Law of Moses, the Sermon on the Mount deals with the attitudes of the heart, in addition to the actions of the body. Here are the beatitudes of Christ as found in Matthew 5:3-10:

The Beatitudes

Blessed are the poor in spirit, for theirs is the kingdom of heaven.

Blessed are those who mourn, for they will be comforted.

Blessed are the meek, for they will inherit the earth.

Blessed are those who hunger and thirst for righteousness, for they will be filled.

Blessed are the merciful, for they will be shown mercy.

Blessed are the pure in heart, for they will see God.

Blessed are the peacemakers, for they will be called children of God.

Blessed are those who are persecuted because of righteousness, for theirs is the kingdom of heaven.

Jesus taught that people should be humble in their souls and sad about their sins. He explained that those who are going to be part of God's future kingdom should have certain inner qualities while they live on this earth such as mercy, purity of heart, a hunger and thirst for righteousness, and a desire to promote peace between all men and peace between men and God. God's standard of beauty includes the willingness to endure suffering with patience.

How do your attitudes measure up to the standards that Jesus presents? What does your soul reflect when looking into *this* mirror?

After giving the Beatitudes in the Sermon on the Mount, Jesus reminded his audience that he did come not to abolish Moses' Law, but to perfectly *fulfill* it. Jesus used the Beatitudes in his Sermon on the Mount to up the ante on the Ten Commandments. **By adding perfect attitudes to the required perfect behaviors given by Moses, Jesus established that God's standard of holiness includes flawless thoughts *and* actions.** Jesus said, for example, that in addition to not murdering someone, you should also never be unjustly angry with another person. *"But I tell you that anyone who is angry with his brother will be subject to judgment."* (Matthew 5:22) The root of murder is the emotion of anger. Another example was that you not only should avoid adultery, you should never lust a person in your mind or heart. Lust is the attitude that leads to adultery. You get the point. This is another reminder that your thoughts control your actions. God's standard of perfect beauty is seen in Jesus Christ because both Jesus' thoughts and actions completely followed both the Ten Commandments and the Beatitudes. Jesus is perfectly beautiful.

Jesus summed up God's Laws and the Beatitudes by stating that we should love God and love people, perfectly. If we could do this, we would never sin. Love conquers sin. If you can do this, you are eternally beautiful and you perfectly reflect God's image in your life.

Perhaps this discussion has led you to despair. The spiritual mirror is trustworthy and accurate, but it is revealing flaws in your character. Does your soul look bad in this mirror? If so, this is *exactly* what Jesus is trying to get you to realize. **Jesus wants you to see your sin, the ugliness of your soul, so that you will be driven to him for salvation and transformation.**

The Bible shows us that if we break the Law of God, or even have an attitude that leads to breaking the Law, we are worthy of death. Uh oh. We are all doomed. We do not naturally have the attributes of God's personality in us. Being like God is *impossible* without God's help. Jesus says, *"With man this is impossible, but with God all things are possible."* (Matthew 19:26) We must be transformed into His likeness.

Jesus came to die the death that we deserved. He kept the Law and the Beatitudes perfectly, never sinning against God or man in his thoughts or actions, so He was the perfect sacrifice for our sinful behaviors. Jesus did for us what we could not do for ourselves. This is the good news of the gospel.

Under the forgiveness that we receive from Jesus, we can look into the mirror of Scripture, realize that we are helpless to change without God, and then begin to yield to God's Spirit within us to take baby steps towards Christ-likeness. We want to end up looking like Jesus. It is going to be a process. It will be a journey taken one day at a time, one step at a time, one moment at a time.

As we walk this path of spiritual transformation, each passing year will have us glancing into the mirror and finding that we are beginning to reflect attitudes and actions that look more and more like our brother, Jesus, and our Heavenly Father, God. The family resemblance will begin to show, if we are faithful to look each day into God's spiritual mirror, the Bible.

Be Intentional

- Start reading the Bible daily in order to look at yourself based on what the Bible says.

- Create a daily Bible reading schedule to follow.

- Daily Schedules can be found at http://www.oneyearbibleonline.com

- If you would like to also read a daily commentary that takes you through the One Year Bible, you can read my One Year Bible Commentary online at http://www.myyearofjubilee50.blogspot.com

Questions for Personal Reflection or Group Study

- How is the Bible a trusty mirror that is able to reflect the condition of your soul?

- How do the Ten Commandments and the Beatitudes act as part of that mirror?

- Why does Jesus want you to see the ugliness of your soul as seen in the mirror of Scripture?

- What is this mirror reflecting to you about your soul?

Day Six
Your Personal Makeover

A Jewel of Transformation: The Bible is your spiritual mirror.

A Verse to Claim: *"If you look carefully into God's perfect law that sets you free, and if you do what it says and don't forget what you heard, then God will bless you for doing it."* (James 1:25)

A Question to Ponder: What does God's mirror reflect back to me about my spiritual beauty?

Makeover Tip to Implement: On a sticky note write out one of the Beatitudes that you want reflected in your character. Place that sticky note on your mirror to remind yourself of this spiritual goal this week. Write in your ESM journal about your desire to develop this character quality and how God can help you accomplish that.

Day 7
Embracing Self Examination

Behavior is the mirror in which everyone shows their image.

~Johann Wolfgang von Goethe

We have established that the Bible is your spiritual mirror. It is through this mirror that you are able to determine the condition of your soul. This may seem like a simple proposition, but sometimes we tend to avoid dealing with our flaws. As an Extreme Spiritual Makeover candidate, you must be willing to look into the mirror of the Bible to examine yourself, identifying attitudes and actions that require transformation, and asking God to help you make changes.

Finding the Courage to Look

The Bible says, *"The heart is deceitful above all things,*

and desperately wicked: who can know it?" (Jeremiah 17:9) (KJV) For this reason, it is important to steel your resolve to examine yourself truthfully. Do you have bad attitudes towards God and others? Are you overly critical of others? Perhaps, you are unrealistically critical of yourself. Do you realize that constant self-criticism is sinful? Maybe you are clinging to a habitual sin in your life and you are unwilling to let go. Looking each day at the Bible will help you identify problem areas.

A King Who was Willing to Look

The Bible provides an excellent example of someone who was willing to look into the mirror of Scripture and make changes based on the ugliness the mirror reflected back to him. His name was Josiah, and he inherited the throne of the Southern Kingdom of Israel when he was only eight years old. His rule came about at a time when the nation of Israel had neglected the Law and fallen away from God. The leaders and the people never looked into the mirror of God's Word.

As a result, the people's thoughts and actions had become very evil. They completely forgot the God who had brought them out of slavery in Egypt, worshiping wooden idols and pagan gods instead. They also had become sexually immoral, incorporating pagan sexual rituals into their worship.

When he turned sixteen, Josiah rejected the pagan worship of his nation and began to seek the God of David, his ancestor. By the time he was twenty years old, Josiah destroyed all of the pagan shrines and worship poles in the kingdom. Josiah felt in his heart that it was wrong to worship other gods, so he personally smashed altars, broke fertility poles, and scattered broken idols over the graves of those who had taken part in the worship of these false gods.

As part of his clean-up effort, Josiah decided to repair the Temple originally built to worship the true God of Israel. While working at the Temple, the High Priest found the book of the Law of Moses, including the Ten Commandments, amongst the ruins. Remember, the Ten Commandments are part of what we just studied in Day Six. These Scriptures had been lost in the crumbled remains of the building.

The High Priest gave the sacred Scriptures to King Josiah's secretary, who brought it before the king to be read. When the king heard the words of the Law for the first time, he tore his robe in sorrow and despair. The Scriptures revealed how ugly the souls of the people of Israel had become after years of ignoring the Word of God. It was obvious to Josiah how far they had fallen from God's holy standard.

God's Law contained promises that were unique to the Jewish people detailing that they were the chosen people through whom the Savior of the world would come. With this in mind, King Josiah had the whole book of the Covenant read out loud to his whole kingdom. Josiah personally insured that his people looked into the mirror of God's Word because he wanted them to be confronted with God's holiness and their own spiritual ugliness. He was courageously willing to look into the mirror of Scripture and make a change. Under Josiah's leadership, the nation of Israel renewed their covenant with God and turned from sin to restore proper worship.

Josiah was a man willing to look into the mirror and examine his life based on God's standards. Feeling convicted about his shortcomings, he confessed his own sins, as well as the sins of his people, asked God for forgiveness, and took steps to correct the situation. Josiah was a beautiful person. Josiah experienced an Extreme Spiritual Makeover and led his kingdom to experience a makeover, too.

Remembering What You Saw

Self-examination means being honest with how your attitudes and actions compare to God's Word. Does the Bible tell you to love people, but really you hate them? Does the Bible ask you not to gossip, but you just can't resist listening to the latest dirt from one of your friends? When you read the truth of Scripture, are you convicted about your behavior, but you choose to walk away from the mirror and forget what you saw in yourself? Do you read the Bible, but set it down, dismissing from your mind what it said?

In your Extreme Spiritual Makeover, daily self-examination is key. Don't you look intently into your regular mirror each morning to see how you look? Would you really walk out the door on any given day if when you checked yourself in the mirror you saw that you had lipstick on your teeth?

Looking into God's mirror each day is just as essential to developing your inner beauty as looking into a physical mirror is for maintaining your physical beauty. You cannot transform your inner person without checking the mirror of Scripture each day. Look into that mirror and make that change.

Just Do It

The Nike Company has become famous for their ad campaign, *"Just Do It."* One of Jesus' disciples would have loved this ad campaign because his writings follow the same principle. James, the half brother of Jesus, was a leader in the early Church. In his letter to believers, James encourages us to act upon what we believe. James wants people to read God's Word and, like King Josiah, *do* something about it.

In James 1:22-24 it says, *"Do not merely listen to the Word, and deceive yourselves. Do what it says. If anyone listens to the word but does not do what it says, he is like a man who looks at his face in the mirror and, after looking at himself, goes away and immediately forgets what he looks like."*

This is critical in your Extreme Spiritual Makeover. **You must *do* what Scripture tells you to do.** You must confess your sins and adjust any wrong attitudes. The good news is that you don't have to make these changes on your own. You can be transformed with the help of God's Spirit inside of you. **It is not your will power, but the power of God's Spirit in you that makes the change possible.**

Why not commit right now to reading the Bible daily? Use the Bible as a mirror to examine your life. As you see flaws in yourself, why not confess your sins, and ask God to transform your attitudes and actions to reflect His love in and through you?

Be Intentional

- Read Galatians 5:16-21. List out actions and attitudes that may apply to your life that are listed in these verses.

- Now, write out some opposing attitudes that you should adopt that reflect God's image.

- Purpose to rely on God's Holy Spirit to fill you with the ability to practice godly attitudes in your life today and to discard the ungodly attitudes.

- Write about your experience doing this.

Questions for Personal Reflection or Group Study

- Why does this Scripture, *"The heart is deceitful above all things, and desperately wicked: who can know it?"*

Embracing Self Examination

(Jeremiah 17:9) promote the idea that daily self-examination is important?

- How does this relate to becoming more spiritually beautiful?

- What do you find impressive about Josiah's story?

- How does the passage from James relate to the Nike theme and to becoming more beautiful like Christ?

Day Seven
Your Personal Makeover

A Jewel of Transformation: Look into the mirror and make that change.

A Verse to Claim: *"Do what it says."* (James 1:22)

A Question to Ponder: What wrong attitude or behavior can I begin to change today?

Makeover Tip to Implement: On a separate piece of paper, write down one sinful attitude that you have that you know God hates. Crinkle up that paper and throw it in the trash. Commit to throwing that attitude out of your life. In your ESM journal, list attitudes and actions that you intend to change over time and with God's help. Make sure to date this page so that you can go back at a later date and see how you have changed.

Exfoliating Sin

If you do what is right, will you not be accepted?

But if you do not do what is right,

sin is crouching at your door;

it desires to have you,

but you must master it.

~Genesis 4:7

Day 8

Rubbing Out Rubbish

Jesus is like any good fisherman, first, He catches the fish; then, He cleans them.

~Mark Potter

Skin is the largest organ in the human body. Most people don't think of skin as an organ; we usually think of it as, well, *skin*. But this oft-ignored organ is incredibly important to our survival. Not only does it cover our bones and muscles, it prevents bacteria and viruses from getting into our bodies, and also helps to regulate body temperature. While we tend to only value it as part of our appearance, this organ is as important to our survival as our heart. Therefore, any good makeover should include a skin care treatment. Because skin is constantly replenishing itself, dead cells on its surface slough off as new cells grow underneath. As part of a good beauty regimen, we should exfoliate dead skin cells by applying mildly abrasive materials to the skin.

As part of your Extreme Spiritual Makeover, you must exfoliate something that covers the whole of human existence in this fallen world: sin. Day Seven encouraged you to read the Bible daily to identify sin in your life. Sin is like dead skin cells, covering every aspect of you. In order to be spiritually healthy, you must exfoliate the sin in your life each day to experience transformation. What sinful behaviors are covering your life? What areas of your life need to be scrubbed off and washed away?

Do you remember the story of Pinocchio? In the Disney version, Pinocchio's creator, Geppetto, longs for a child and wishes on a wishing star that his puppet would become a real boy. When he goes to bed that night, a Blue Fairy grants his wish, bringing Pinocchio to life. Because Pinocchio is not a real boy, but a wooden puppet, albeit a living one, the fairy provides him with a mentor named Jiminy Cricket, who acts as Pinocchio's conscience, helping him to distinguish right from wrong. Adventure ensues as Pinocchio is exposed to evil and confronts his own tendency to do wrong. Whenever Pinocchio lies, his nose grows longer. Remember his shocked look as his nose exposed his lies? Pinocchio's sin had a physical consequence.

What if your sins had physical consequences the way Pinocchio's lying did? What would you look like if each time you lied, your nose grew a quarter of an inch? What about worrying? If you got a worrywart every time you worried about something instead of praying about your anxiety, would you be covered in warts right now? What if every time you spoke angrily to someone when you were stressed out, some of your hair would fall out? Would you be bald at this point?

If your sins had physical consequences like Pinocchio's, there would be no hiding your faults. You would probably be far more diligent in exfoliating your sin. Although many of your sins are not visible to others, their impact on your soul is just as real. The secrecy of hidden sin allows you to appear one way on the outside, while being quite different on the inside.

In order to become spiritually beautiful like Christ, you have to exfoliate sin from your life. But doing so is a process, not a one-time event. Our skin is constantly regenerating. Each day, more surface cells die and need to be removed. Similarly, being human, we sin every day. We need to treat sin in our lives the same way we treat dead skin, by exfoliating it daily. Until we are free of our earthly bodies, we will continue to sin and we must be vigilant, persistently rubbing out sin.

In Day Six, we talked about the need to use the Bible as a spiritual mirror in order to see the ugliness of sin in our souls. Now, we need to find ways to rub out the sin that we have identified. Dealing with our faults is not pleasant work, but two truths should motivate us to do this exfoliation each day: God hates sin and God forgives sin. Let's take a closer look at both of these truths.

God Hates Sin

One motivation for exfoliating sin each day is that God hates sin. Sin is what separates you from fellowship with God. God is holy and sin is not part of His image. This is not to say that God hates us if we sin. God is gracious and compassionate and provides a solution for the punishment that sin demands, but if we embrace sin in our lives, it acts as a barrier to our relationship with God. If you want to have close fellowship with your Creator and bring glory to Him, you must constantly work to eliminate sin in your life. This is a life-long process. One motivation for steadily working to rub out sin is to adopt God's attitude about sin, which is that He hates sin, not the sinner. As an Extreme Spiritual Makeover candidate, each day you are to wash off the sinful attitudes and actions that prevent you from being close to God and from loving other people. You must hate the sin in your life, but not hate yourself for the mistakes you make. This may sound crazy, but it is possible.

On a grand scale, we can see God's hatred of sin when He eliminated the sin that had covered and polluted the planet prior the Great Flood. The Bible tells us that only Noah and his family were found righteous on the earth (Genesis 6-9). Similarly, when the cities of Sodom and Gomorrah became decadent, God rained down fire and brimstone, exfoliating these cities and their inhabitants from the face of the earth with only Lot and his daughters surviving (Genesis 19). Even in the early

Church, Ananias and Sapphira were struck dead when they lied to the Holy Spirit (Acts 5). God is deadly serious about exfoliating sin, and you should be, too.

It is important to distinguish between how God treats those who have humbly repented from their sins through faith in God (the righteous) and those who pridefully rebel against God and are unrepentant about their sin (the unrighteous). God always preserved the righteous people in these exfoliation stories. They were declared righteous if they loved God and had turned to Him in faith. Being righteous caused their preservation in judgment and they were not punished with the wicked, even though they were not individually perfect and without sin in their lives. God's intention was to make a strong statement in each case about how He despised unrepentant sin and prideful rebellion against Him. God does not expect perfection from us, but He does expect repentance from sin.

As a makeover candidate, you must despise any sin that you find within yourself and rub it out as it crops up each day, so that as you repent of your errors, your humility is evident to God.

God Forgives Sin

Another motivation for exfoliating the sin in our lives is that God forgives our sins. If we have trusted in Christ, God embraces our membership in His family and delights in loving and communing with us. Our gratitude to

God for forgiving us of our past, present, and future sins is a wonderful motivation to begin to identify those sins for which we have been forgiven and rub them out of our lives. The Bible says, *"Blessed is the man whose sin the Lord does not count against him and in whose spirit is no deceit."* (Psalm 32:2) So let's get rid of sinful attitudes and behaviors in gratitude for what Christ has done for us!

There is a beautiful story of forgiveness in the Bible in John chapter eight. Jesus was in the Temple teaching the people when the Pharisees brought him a woman who had been caught in adultery. The leaders sought to test Jesus saying, *"Now in the Law Moses commanded us to stone such women; what then do you say?"* (John 8:5)

Rather than stepping in their trap, Jesus ignored them and began writing something in the dirt. As he wrote, everybody was waiting to hear his response. When the Pharisees pressed him for an answer, he stood up, looked her accusers in the eyes and said, *"If any one of you is without sin, let him be the first to throw a stone at her."* (John 8:7) Then, he stooped down and continued writing in the dirt. Sometimes, I like to speculate that he was writing the Ten Commandments in the dirt for all of the Pharisees and the teachers of the Law to ponder!

One by one, everyone left the scene until Jesus was left alone with the woman. Jesus was the only person who could legitimately stone the woman, because He was the only person in that crowd who had never sinned. But, Jesus did *not* stone the woman. He *forgave* her. At this point, Jesus asked the woman where all of her accusers had gone. *"Has no one condemned you?" "No one, sir," she replied. "Then neither do I condemn you," Jesus declared. "Go and leave your life of sin."* (John 8:10-11)

Notice that Jesus tells the woman to leave her life of sin. Jesus is asking this woman to exfoliate the sin of adultery from her life. She does not have permission to live in constant sin after being forgiven. Jesus expects her to be filled with gratitude for being spared from death, and to *change* as a result of her love and gratitude to God for saving her. This woman is expected to undergo an Extreme Spiritual Makeover after her encounter with Christ.

Lessons

You are in the same position as the woman caught in adultery. You, too, must exfoliate the sin in your life. **Whether you are motivated by the knowledge that God hates sin or by feelings of gratefulness for having been forgiven, Jesus expects you to *"go and leave your life of sin."*** Now, let's discuss *how* to exfoliate sin.

The Exfoliation Technique

The Bible teaches in 1 John 1:9 that there is a spiritual process for exfoliating sin from your life. It says, *"If we confess our sins, he is faithful and just and will forgive us our sins and purify us from all unrighteousness."* **You must confess your sins to be cleansed.** The process of exfoliating sin includes identifying sin in your life through daily Bible reading and honest reflection. After honest reflection, you are to confess what you have done wrong. Next, you must apply an abrasive to loosen the hold of sin on your life. It is not easy to let go of wrong attitudes, bad habits, and natural desires. There are tools available that will facilitate the exfoliation (spiritual loofahs) such as accountability groups, prayer groups, Christian radio programs that teach truth, and regular church attendance. As you discipline yourself to exfoliate sin each day, you will gradually become a person filled with eternal beauty. This will give you the freedom to not return to your life of sin.

Be Intentional

- List sins that you believe God hates that you are guilty of doing. Do you also hate those sins? Why?

- Ask a friend to keep you accountable. You will need to tell that friend some of the sins you are working to exfoliate daily. Example: You have a problem with gossip. Have your friend call you out when you begin to talk behind someone's back.

- Look up verses on the topic of the sins that are particularly prevalent in your life. Think and meditate on these verses. Memorize them.

- Avoid situations that lead to your particular sin problem. Example: You have the problem of gluttony (over eating). You realize that you eat for emotional reasons. Purpose to pray when you are feeling strong emotions, rather than going to the kitchen to get something to eat.

- Realize that God has forgiven you. Have you forgiven yourself for these sins? Let this forgiveness motivate you to stop the sin.

Questions for Personal Reflection or Group Study

- If your internal sins (ungodly attitudes) popped up physically on your body, what would they look like? How would you feel if this really happened?

- What motives you to stop sinning?

- What are the two motivations for getting rid of sin listed in this chapter?

- Think about some of the exfoliation techniques discussed in this chapter. Which ones might help you to rub out sin in your life?

Day Eight
Your Personal Makeover

A Jewel of Transformation: You must begin to rub sin out of your life.

A Verse to Claim: *"If we confess our sin, he is faithful and just and will forgive us our sins and cleanse us and purify us from all unrighteousness."* (1 John 1:9)

A Question to Ponder: How can I begin to confess my sins and rub them out of my daily life? How can I begin to forgive others for sinning against me?

Makeover Tip to Implement: Think some sins that are hard to overcome. List them in your ESM journal. Now, list situations that lead to these sins. Purpose to avoid triggers that cause you to sin.

Day 9

Liposuctioning Excess

Repent then, and turn to God,

so that your sins may be wiped out,

that times of refreshing may come from the Lord.

~Acts 3:19

No good makeover on television is complete without the candidate receiving a procedure called liposuction. You've seen it. A cosmetic surgeon basically uses a vacuum to suck out unwanted fat. In one afternoon the effects of a lifetime of bad eating habits can be sucked away, restoring a slimmer, more attractive appearance. But unless the patient actually changes their eating habits, in time, the effect of the procedure will be overcome by newly acquired, unwanted fat.

We all know that carrying around too much fat can lead to heart disease, diabetes, and a host of other health problems. As an Extreme Spiritual Makeover candidate, you need to be aware that the excesses in your life can have the same damaging effect on your soul that excessive fat can have on your body. It is important to recognize that excesses in your life may be an indication that you have heart attitudes rooted in sin that need to be "liposuctioned" out of your life. Excesses such as materialism, alcoholism, drug use, addictions to shopping, entertainment, and pornography will keep you from intimacy with God.

Personal Sins

Who among us does not know someone who has fallen into drug or alcohol addiction? Our culture is filled with broken people trapped in the grip of substance abuse. From politicians to musicians, athletes and actors, and even our own family members, the cultural landscape is littered with the bodies of those who have succumbed to addiction. Why is addiction such a big problem for people?

Addiction comes about because we rely on something other than God and biblical principles to deal with the problems and hurts we encounter in life. For example, a person may have suffered the trauma of having been abused in their childhood. The emotional scars and painful memories are so great that the person turns to alcohol to numb the pain and escape the deep sorrow. What starts with an occasional glass of wine at dinner becomes a nightly ritual of several glasses. Over time, an addiction develops, leaving the person unable to face their pain without the sedative effect of alcohol. We have established that in this fallen world, we will *all* endure trials and suffering. The question becomes how can you cope with your pain in a healthy way?

The Bible teaches that you must learn to face and feel your pain. Think of this as *living in the truth*. Jesus says, *"Then you will know the truth, and the truth will set you free."* (John 8:32) Whatever your truth is, whether it is a past abuse, a dysfunctional family, or a divorce, facing your pain and feeling your pain are essential if you want to conquer your pain. Did someone hurt you and it feels impossible to admit it and even more impossible to forgive them? Were you born into a dysfunctional family that left you feeling emotionally abandoned? Admitting what went wrong and realizing that it has caused you pain is the first step in conquering the pain. Your pain is a blessing from God because the pain causes you to realize that you have a problem, and you need a solution to your problem. You need to put away the pride that causes you to want to rely on yourself to cope with the problem and instead turn to God for healing. Instead of relying on unhealthy coping mechanisms that can lead to addiction, you must turn to God to help you deal with your pain. As Adrian Rogers said in his sermon, *The Purposes of Pain*, "You need a Savior, not a sedative." Facing your pain and feeling your pain lead to relying on God to relieve your pain.

Jesus modeled the importance of facing and feeling pain, rather than running from it, when he prayed fervently

in the Garden of Gethsemane prior to his crucifixion. Under the incredible stress of knowing that it was God's will that he carry the weight of the world's past, present, and future sins as he hung on the cross, Jesus' sweat became like great drops of blood. Jesus was trying to cope with the separation he would experience when God would turn His face away from him as he bore our sins on the cross. Some people feel that Jesus was dreading his physical suffering. While the physical aspects of his arrest, beatings, and crucifixion would be torturous, the true spiritual devastation of being separated from God, the Father, because of the sins of the world being placed on him at the cross would have been a much greater horror to face.

The Bible tells us Jesus said, *"'Father, if you are willing, take this cup from me; yet not my will, but your will be done.' An angel from heaven appeared to him and strengthened him. And being in anguish, he prayed more earnestly, and his sweat was like drops of blood falling to the ground."* (Luke 22:42-44)

Can you feel the anxiety and dread in Jesus' words? Do you sense his humility in his willingness to face his fears and not run from this trial? Jesus could have spent these last days having a few drinks with friends in an effort to deaden the reality of what was about to happen to him. But Jesus decides to spend time facing the situation, feeling the pain, and praying in order to seek God's will in this difficult situation. **Jesus was willing to live in his truth.** The truth was that he was born *into* this world to die *for* this world. Jesus relies on His Father to help him battle through the stress of his mission. This takes courage. This takes resolve. This takes faith.

Christ's prayers give him perspective and purpose. Living in the truth of his situation helps Jesus conquer the pain of that situation. *Jesus is our example of what the image of God looks like in a human body.* Do you want to be eternally beautiful? If so, be willing to face and feel your pain like Jesus did. Turn to God with your problems rather than trying to avoid or escape them.

God is there to help you cope with the pain of living in a fallen world. Learning to cope with pain and sorrow in a healthy way requires acknowledging that God is in control of your life. Most successful recovery programs like Alcoholics Anonymous are based on this premise. Reliance upon God is a key to healthy and beautiful living. *"If God is for us, who can be against us? He who did not spare his own Son, but gave him up for us all—how will he not also, along with him, graciously give us all things?"* (Romans 8:31-33) This is a comforting truth. With this truth, one can begin to face, feel, and overcome life's pain.

God uses individuals and organizations to help us begin to liposuction excesses out of our lives. One such individual is Nancy Alcorn. In 1983, Nancy Alcorn started Mercy Ministries in Louisiana. Her vision was to have a faith-based residential program for young women dealing with life-controlling issues such as eating disorders, self-harm, drug and alcohol addictions, depression, and unplanned pregnancy. Using proven methods and a holistic approach that includes reliance upon God and daily Bible reading to receive healing and truth, Mercy Ministries has helped thousands of young women find freedom from sin and addictions. How are their transformations possible? By learning to face and feel the pain of their broken lives and by trusting God to heal the hurts, these women see that God can redeem what was lost. Mercy helps these women liposuction excesses out of their lives by depending on God to heal their pain.

God's love is able to conquer the trials and heartbreaks in this world. As a matter of fact, God wants to be involved in your life by healing your hurts and redeeming your story. The Bible encourages us with these words,

> *No, in all these things we are more than conquerors through him who loved us. For I am convinced that neither death nor life, neither angels nor demons, neither the present nor the future, nor any powers, neither height nor depth, nor anything else in all creation, will be able to separate us from the love of God that is in Christ Jesus our Lord.* (Romans 8:37-39)

Knowing that your struggles and trials, even your past sins, cannot separate you from God's love is proof that you can be redeemed from any situation in your life. Not only can you be redeemed, you can conquer the situation and move from being a victim to being a victor, all by the power of God's love.

Societal Sins

In addition to liposuctioning personal excesses out of your life through prayer and turning to God for help, you should begin to honestly evaluate whether society's values are influencing you. Do you find that social norms that have been put forth by the culture and media have begun to shape your sense of right and wrong? Does what your culture thinks is acceptable square with God's Word? For example, it has become alarmingly common for couples to live together without getting married. They are even having children outside of wedlock. Has this shift in society's values influenced you to compromise your sexual integrity? Do you ever stand up against these societal shifts and take a stand for the truth?

Taking a Stand

The Bible tells the story of one man who had to take a stand against his culture and stand up for God. His name was Noah. Back in Noah's day, the earth had become incredibly wicked. Scripture tells us, "The Lord saw how great man's wickedness on the earth had become, and that every inclination of the thoughts of his heart was only evil all the time. The Lord was grieved that he had made man on the earth, and his heart was filled with pain." (Genesis 6:5-6) Noah lived at a time when it got so bad that God decided to step in eliminate the excesses of sin upon the earth.

The story of the Great Flood is the story of God liposuctioning societal sin from the earth. The fat of evil was infecting the heart of mankind, so God wiped out this excessive evil in order to preserve the human race. Only Noah and his family were found to be righteous. Remember, we learned that righteousness is a position that is determined by one's faith. The Bible says, "The Lord then said to Noah, 'Go into the ark, you and your whole family, because I have found you righteous in this generation.'" (Genesis 7:1)

Noah stood up for what he believed in the face of an evil generation. He was a man of faith who, in building the ark, acted out of obedience. His righteous thoughts resulted in righteous behavior. Noah trusted God, entered the ark as commanded, and he and his family were saved from the waters of God's judgment.

Can you see the parallels in what Noah experienced and what we experience when we trust Jesus? We have to trust that Christ saves us from God's judgment against sin, just as Noah had to trust that the ark would save him from the judgment that was the Great Flood. The beauty of Noah's faith was seen in his righteous attitudes and actions, just as your faith is seen through your attitudes and actions.

Be Beautiful Where You Are

Liposuctioning sin from your life will make you more beautiful in your soul. Learning to face and feel your pain is the beginning of learning to live in truth. When you live in truth, you become honest about your life. When you see your own life clearly, you begin to see the truth about society more clearly. This clarity leads to taking a stand against cultural norms that go against God's standards. You will be salt and light in a world that needs preservation and illumination because your inner beauty and transformation will cause you to think God's thoughts and live out God's will on earth. Now that is beauty that lasts!

Be Intentional

- Do an inventory of your life as an exercise for living in truth. Rate the following areas of your life from 1-10 with 10 being very good: family, work, health, financial, spiritual, charitable, relationships, hobbies, adventure, travel, dreams and ambitions

- List past hurts in your life.

- List ways you have hurt others in the past.

- Purpose to realize that what is past is over. Do not wish for the past to be different.

- Ask God for the strength to accept the past as it is.

- Grieve for what is past, openly and honestly.

- Release any bitterness the past is causing you. Forgive those who have hurt you.

- Ask forgiveness in your heart for the ways you have hurt others. Forgive yourself for the ways that you have hurt others. Thanking God for all of it.

- Realize that all things work together for good for those who love God and are called according to His purpose. (Romans 8:28)

Questions for Personal Reflection or Group Study

- How is addiction tied to self-reliant pride?

- What is Kathy referring to when she says to "live in your truth"?

- What is the purpose of pain?

- How does releasing past pain and bitterness start the process of liposuctioning excesses from your life?

- How will doing this make you more eternally beautiful like Christ?

Day Nine
Your Personal Makeover

A Jewel of Transformation: The best way to cope with pain is humble reliance upon God to help you forgive past hurts and face present trials with faith.

A Verse to Claim: *"In a word, what I'm saying is, Grow up. You're kingdom subjects. Now live like it. Live out your God-created identity. Live generously and graciously toward others, the way God lives toward you."* (Matthew 5:48) (The Message)

A Question to Ponder: How can I humbly face trials like Christ did?

Makeover Tip to Implement: Find someone who needs to be encouraged to rely on God, rather than relying on a bad habit to cope. Write a note of encouragement to them and send it out today.

If that person is you, write a note of encouragement to yourself in your ESM Journal.

Nutrition - Food for the Soul

How sweet are your words to my taste,

sweeter than honey to my mouth.

~Psalm 119:103

Day 10

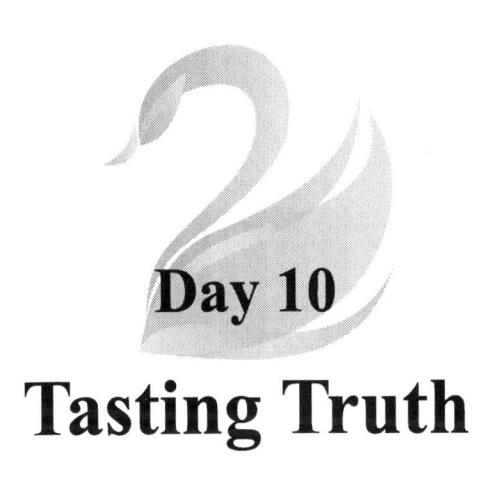

Tasting Truth

I am the bread of life.

He who comes to me will never go hungry.

Whoever believes in me will never be thirsty.

~John 6:23

    As long as there have been humans on the earth, there has been comfort food. Archeologists have found artifacts from the year 6000 BC that show our ancestors dining on hippopotamus soup. It's not exactly mac 'n cheese, but they probably saw it as the ultimate comfort food. Our meals bring so much pleasure and comfort that it is easy to forget that food is the fuel that keeps our bodies alive. Our bodies derive energy from our food, just as cars derive energy from gasoline. Raw materials, including amino acids and calcium, nourish, build, and repair our cells. Little helpers, such as phytochemicals and antioxidants, prevent inflammation and can actually heal your body by consuming free radicals that cause cell damage. The fact that our daily provisions fuel, build, and heal our bodies should motivate us to eat a proper diet. If we begin to think about our meals in this way, food can represent more to us than just pleasure and comfort, it can be appreciated as a lifeline.

Just as physical food is important to our bodies and affects our emotional and physical health, spiritual food is important to our spiritual health. What you put into your mind fuels your spiritual life and sustains your soul.

God as our Provider

When little babies start their lives, they need to eat every four hours. I remember as a first time mother scheduling my day around when my baby would need to be fed. It seemed that just when I had finished feeding him, he would take a brief nap, get his diaper changed, and be ready to eat all over again. Although exhausting, meeting my child's needs brought me so much joy and pleasure. Love overwhelmed my life as I provided for my child so that he could grow. This is how God feels about you. His love for you is all consuming. He delights in meeting your spiritual needs.

As an Extreme Spiritual Makeover candidate, from the minute you were born again, God was keenly interested in nourishing you so that you would grow and develop into His image. Remember, you are a soul, so God is interested in nourishing you. As we develop and grow in our spiritual lives, God is like a nursing mother who nourishes our hunger to be like Him. *"Can a mother forget the baby at her breast and have no compassion on the child she has borne? Though she may forget, I will not forget you!"* (Isaiah 49:15) If God is like our nursing mother, then we should be like hungry babies, crying out to be fed. We must yearn for His provisions.

Food in the Desert

God often uses physical realities to teach us spiritual truths. The sixteenth chapter of Exodus preserves the story of how God provided for the Israelites' physical needs in order to teach them (and us) to look to Him to satisfy their spiritual needs, as well. After freeing them from slavery in Egypt, God led the Israelites into the desert en route to the Promised Land. But life in the desert was hard, and food was not as plentiful as it had been in Egypt. Like babies that had missed a feeding, the people began to cry out against Moses, even questioning whether they would have been better off had they remained slaves in Egypt. Moses' leadership was under assault.

God stepped into the situation to provide for His people's physical needs, while teaching them a spiritual truth. Demonstrating His love, God literally rained down bread from heaven. Every morning, God provided manna, a sweet, flaky substance like bread, that the people gathered. When the Israelites grumbled that they also wanted meat to eat, God caused quail to descend upon the camp, so they would have meat for dinner. God provided manna and quail for His people every day for forty years. God was faithful to provide for the needs of His people.

In feeding the Israelites, God was doing much more than just meeting a physical need. As Moses explains in the book of Deuteronomy, *"He humbled you, causing you to hunger and then feeding you with manna, which neither you nor your fathers had known, to teach you that man does not live on bread alone but on every word that comes from the mouth of the Lord."* (Deuteronomy 8:3) God's greater purpose was to teach that it is His Word that sustains our souls and strengthens our spirits.

Moses' words in Deuteronomy may seem familiar because these are the very words that Jesus spoke to Satan after Jesus had been fasting for forty days and nights in the wilderness. In Matthew 4:1-4, we read,

> *Then Jesus was led by the Spirit into the desert to be tempted by the devil. After fasting forty days and forty nights, he was hungry. The tempter came to him and said, 'If you are the Son of God, tell these stones to become bread.' Jesus answered, It is written: 'Man does not live by bread alone, but on every word that comes from the mouth of God.'*

Jesus is showing us in this passage that it is the truth of God's Word that keeps us alive spiritually. It is the truth of His Word that fuels us to grow into an eternally beautiful person like Jesus. We must base our faith upon and build our lives upon this truth. An essential element of that truth is that it is Jesus who saves us from our sins and restores our relationship with God. Jesus is our lifeline. We must feed ourselves on this truth from His Word, every day.

Are You Full or Starving?

You are what you eat.

~Anonymous

Jesus shows us that in order to be to be spiritually healthy, we need to feed our souls by consuming God's Word each day. It behooves us to examine whether we are really eating a healthy spiritual diet.

There is a lot of truth in the saying, "You are what you eat." If you feed your body a steady diet of junk food, your health will eventually suffer. It is equally important to be conscious of what you are feeding your mind. Just as your body must be fed with healthy food to keep fueled, nourished, and healed, your mind must be fed with truth on a daily basis to thrive and grow. Think back over the last month. How often have you gone for days without any spiritual food? Have you been depriving yourself of essential spiritual nutrition, instead gorging on spiritual junk food? Are you essentially spiritually anorexic?

Here is a scenario of a woman who claims to love God and believe in Jesus. See what you think of her spiritual diet.

> *Joyce had a steady diet. Each morning she flipped on the radio to hear a local psychic as she drank her coffee and made sack lunches for the kids. Once everyone was off to school, Joyce read her horoscope in the paper before turning on her favorite morning talk show on TV. Next, she ran errands and returned in time to watch her favorite soap opera. After picking up the kids from school, Joyce turned on The Real Housewives of Atlanta, which was constantly running on one of the cable channels, while she cooked dinner. Putting the kids to bed was the precursor for a little down time with her favorite romance novel.*

We must be discerning when it comes to what we put in our minds. It is actually possible to either starve yourself by never reading God's Word or to pollute yourself by filling your heart and mind with ideas that are not beneficial. You must be picky about the kind of nutrition you give your inner person. **Remember that in this life, you are nurturing and developing your eternal person.**

Just as you might take the time to read the ingredients on a package of food you are buying to make sure that it is not filled with sugar and sodium, you must analyze what you are feeding your mind each day to see if it is packed with truth or lies. This is of utmost importance. Give yourself spiritual fruit and veggies, rather than candy and pop tarts. Be intentional in what you feed your soul. A steady diet of God's Word is the only thing that will keep you healthy and thriving spiritually.

Jesus as Our Nourishment

The Bible gives many illustrations of God giving food to people because food is so essential to our lives and God is the provider of what is essential to us both physically and spiritually. The truth that God sustains us is what Jesus taught in his desert temptation. He continued this idea when he miraculously fed five thousand people. It is a consistent picture. Jesus is God the Son, so it makes sense that Jesus provides food for the hungry crowd of Israelites, just as God the Father, provided food for the hungry Israelites in the desert. The consistent message is that God provides for His people.

Jesus teaches his disciples that the manna in the desert was a picture of *him*. In John 6:32 Jesus says, *"I tell you the truth, it is not Moses who has given you the bread from heaven, but it is my Father who gives you the true bread from heaven. For the bread of God is he who comes down from heaven and gives life to the world."* Jesus is that life-giving bread from heaven. The story of the Israelites and the manna in the desert was a foreshadowing of the eternal truth that one day, Jesus would come to earth to be the bread that would feed your soul forever. If you partake of Christ, you will live forever.

By portraying himself as the bread from heaven that sustains us, Jesus is saying that he wants us to consume him, in a sense. The Bible says, *" I am the living bread that came down from heaven. If anyone eats of this bread, he will live forever. This bread is my flesh, which will give for the life of the world."* (John 6:51)

Everyday we are to consume the truth about Christ as found in His Word. Doing so is the way to eat a healthy spiritual diet. Jesus also continued this picture of being sustained by him when he instituted the sacrament of communion. By taking communion, you are commemorating what Jesus Christ did. As you eat the bread and drink of the cup, you acknowledge that his death and his resurrected life are what give you spiritual life, forever. What a glorious truth!

In your Extreme Spiritual Makeover, it is essential that you nourish your soul daily with the truth of Jesus Christ. Jesus is the bread that keeps you alive forever. His Word is the food that enables your soul to conform to the image of God. When you conform to His image, you become eternally beautiful.

Be Intentional

- List television shows that may be spiritual junk food to you. Start to eliminate them from your diet.

- List activities that nourish your soul. Try to steadily participate in these activities.

- List people who are negative and bring you down. Create boundaries with these people.

- List situations where God is honored in your life. Create more of these opportunities.

Questions for Personal Reflection or Group Study

- Why is nourishing your soul like feeding a newborn baby or a growing child?

- What does God provide to feed your soul?

- How does this nourish, heal, and preserve you?

- What is your responsibility in all of this?

- Are you full or starving spiritually?

Day 10

Your Personal Makeover

A Jewel of Transformation: Jesus is the bread that keeps your spirit alive forever.

A Verse to Claim: *"I am the bread of life."* (John 6:35)

Question to Ponder: What am I consuming spiritually each day?

Makeover Tip to Implement: Go and buy some of your favorite kind of bread. With purpose and pleasure eat a piece of the bread and thank Jesus that His body was broken for you. Write a prayer of thanksgiving in your ESM journal about how Jesus will keep your spirit and soul alive forever.

Day 11
Fuel To Fight

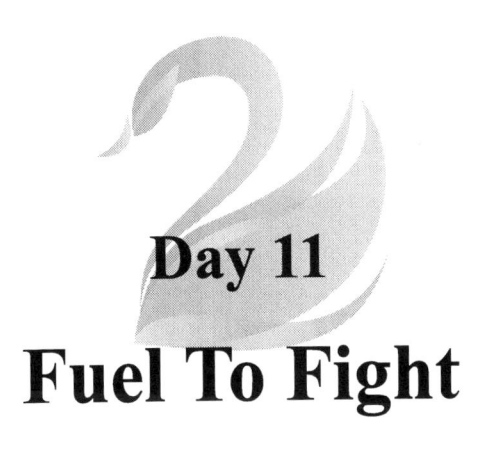

I have food to eat that you know nothing about.

~John 4:32

    In preparation for our annual trip to Florida, my husband and I decided to jointly start a new diet and exercise routine in order to drop a few pounds. The diet that we chose required eating complex carbohydrates, lots of protein, and plenty of fruits and vegetables. We were to have five small meals a day and try to exercise at least thirty minutes each day. My husband had successfully lost 45 pounds on this system before and strongly believed in the principles of the program. I had lost weight before on this system, too, just not as much as him, so I believed in it, too.

    At the start, we were doing well. Both of us had been regulating our eating and exercising daily. At the end of the first week, we were relaxing in our success. It had been a long day, including a walk that lasted over an hour. Our calorie intake was less than we were used to before the diet, but we were coping with the slight hunger just fine. As evening fell, we lounged on the couch and turned on the television to relax. Everything was fine, at first. Then, the television became our enemy. The voice of the tempter relentlessly mocked us, as every other commercial was for some kind of food. Initially, the temptation was mild. There were two or three commercials for pizza showing oozing cheese and crusty crusts that were too rich to really bother us. We weren't in the mood for pizza. Next, was a commercial for a burger joint with camera shots of grilled meat and French fries that assaulted our senses. I must say, those potatoes looked perfectly seasoned and tasty. Did I mention that on this diet you are usually just a little hungry all the time? Our stomachs grumbled as we watched that one. Finally, an ice cream commercial came on. The cool, creamy treats, including a blizzard of toppings were the true test. Could we resist getting off the couch and heading to Dairy Queen?

I am happy to report that our faith in this eating plan and our desire to lose weight trumped the temptation to break the diet. Most of the credit should go to my husband, who acts as the food police around our house. When it came to dieting, his faith and actions influenced my faith and actions. Our faith was like food that fueled us to fight temptation.

Running on Empty

One of the keys to obedience in the Christian life and becoming more beautiful like Christ is learning how to keep fueled so that you are able to fight temptation. If you are out of gas spiritually, it will be very hard for you to avoid succumbing to sin in your life. One way to stay fueled is understand why God allows temptation.

The story of humanity, at least in one respect, is the story of our ancestors being unable to resist temptation. From Adam and Eve, to you and me, and everyone in between, all of mankind has at some point succumbed to temptation. But, why did God allow Satan to tempt Adam and Eve in the first place? J. Vernon McGee has this to say about the situation:

> The question arises: Why the temptation? If we go back to chapters 1 and 2 of Genesis, we find that man was created innocent, but man was not created righteous. **Righteousness is innocence that has been maintained in the presence of temptation.** You see, temptation will either develop or destroy you; it will do one of the two. The Garden of Eden was not a hothouse, and man was not a hothouse plant. **Character must be developed, and it can only be developed in the in the presence of temptation.** Man was created a responsible being, and he was responsible to glorify, to obey, to serve, and to be subject to divine government. (emphasis added).

Temptation is an opportunity for obedience. Simply stated, God allowed Adam and Eve to be tempted in order to give them an opportunity to demonstrate their obedience. Adam and Eve were created with responsibilities. They were responsible for being good stewards of God's creation and for serving, glorifying, and obeying God. But how is one ever truly responsible if they don't actually take and uphold those responsibilities? Being tempted gave Eve the opportunity to be obedient to God and to trust that His plan for her was both good and loving. Eve needed to trust in God's goodness, in His love, and in the veracity of His words. In other words, Eve needed *faith* in God in order to resist temptation.

We all know how Eve held up in the face of temptation. But we need to look closely at her story because we are all tempted in the same way. Genesis chapter three recounts how Satan came in the form of the serpent to test Eve's faith.

> *Now the serpent was more crafty than any of the wild animals the Lord God had made. He said to the woman, "Did God really say 'You must not eat from any tree in the garden?"*
>
> *The woman said to the serpent, "We may eat fruit from the trees in the garden, but God did say, 'You must not eat fruit from the tree that is in the middle of the*

> *garden, and you must not touch it, or you will die.'"*
>
> *"You will not certainly die," the serpent said to the woman. "For God knows that when you eat from it your eyes will be opened, and you will be like God, knowing good and evil."*
>
> *When the woman saw that the fruit of the tree was good for food and pleasing to the eye, and also desirable for gaining wisdom, she took some and ate it. She also gave some to her husband, who was with her, and he ate it. Then the eyes of both of them were opened, and they realized they were naked; so they sewed fig leaves together and made coverings for themselves.* (Genesis 3:1-6)

Our first lesson from this encounter is to note the technique Satan uses to tempt us. 1 John 2:16 provides valuable insight into Satan's methods, *"For everything in the world, the lust of the flesh, the lust of the eyes, and the pride of life comes not from the Father, but from the world."* (1 John 2:16)

It was through the lust of the flesh, the lust of the eyes and the pride of life that Eve was tempted.

The first way that Eve was tempted was through the lust of the flesh. The **lust of the flesh** is when a person wants something that fulfills a natural desire. Eve saw the fruit of the tree, it looked delicious, and so she wanted to eat it. It appealed to her natural desire to eat tasty food. The problem was that God had said that Adam and Eve were not to eat this particular fruit. He had warned Eve that she would die if she ate this food. Eve needed to believe what God said, to trust that God loved her, and that He was telling her the truth. She needed to be willing to obey God. Satan's first temptation appealed to Eve's natural desire to indulge her flesh. Eve knew that she was not to eat of this tree and pointed out to Satan that God had said that if they ate from that tree, *or even touched it,* they would die. Eve, for some unknown reason, felt compelled to add that they were not to even touch the tree. This was not what God said. Eve was adding to the words of God. God only warned that they would die if they ate from the tree. Heeding God's warning would require faith because at this point, nothing had ever died in Paradise, so Eve had never seen death. Eve would have to trust God's word that they would die if she disobeyed. Her knowledge of the truth and her faith in God would have to stop her from acting on this temptation.

The second way in which Eve was tempted was by the lust of the eyes. The **lust of the eyes** is when one desires to have something that is not theirs to have. This is coveting something that does not belong to you. Eve saw that the fruit was attractive. She wanted it, even though God said that it was not hers to eat. To resist this temptation, Eve would need to honor God's will over her own. She would have to put God's desire above her own. Eve would need to trust that God knew it was best that she not eat that fruit, even if she didn't understand why. This would require Eve to have faith in God's goodness and wisdom.

The final temptation was the pride of life. The **pride of life** is a vain craving for honor or recognition. This temptation is an appeal to Eve's ego. Satan told Eve that the only reason God didn't want her to eat from the tree was that He knew that if she did, she would become "like God, knowing good and evil." Satan was appealing to Eve's pride. Listen to his words, *"You will not surely die. For God knows that when you eat of it your eyes will be opened, and you will be like God."* (Genesis 3:4-5) This was heady stuff. Who wouldn't want to be like God? Satan was encouraging Eve to question the love and goodness of God's law. Was God just depriving Eve of something because He was a cosmic killjoy? Why was God preventing Eve from realizing her full potential? Was God threatened by Eve's ability to be like Him? Eve would have to have faith in God's goodness and love in order to resist this temptation.

We all know how this story ended. Eve did *not* obey the one rule that God put in place, choosing to satisfy the lust of the flesh, the lust of the eyes, and her own pride, rather than trust in God. Eve did not have the fuel to fight temptation. Her faith was not strong. Not only did Eve fall to temptation, she dragged her husband down with her. Eve was running on empty and, apparently, Adam was, too.

Eve is an example to us that failing to trust in the truth of God's Word to sustain us in the face of temptation is a recipe for disaster. Eve squandered the opportunity that her temptation presented. She could have demonstrated her righteousness, but instead, she revealed her sinfulness. Thankfully, Jesus Christ gives us an example of how to fuel up with God's Word and fight temptation. Jesus took his temptation as an opportunity to reveal that he was righteous.

Fueled to Fight Temptation

Jesus' experience in the wilderness stands in sharp contrast to Eve's experience in the Garden of Eden. While Eve was in a perfect environment, even personally walking with God when she fell to temptation, Jesus faced Satan's temptations alone in the harsh wilderness.

Unlike Eve, who had been eating plenty of fresh fruits and vegetables in the Garden of Eden prior to her temptation, Jesus had been fasting for forty days and forty nights prior to his confrontation with the devil. Whereas Eve was satisfied physically, while starving and weak spiritually, Jesus was starving physically, while very full and strong spiritually.

The Bible says,

> But he said to me, "My grace is sufficient for you, for my power is made perfect in weakness." Therefore I will boast all the more gladly about my weaknesses, so that Christ's power may rest on me. That is why, for Christ's sake, I delight in weaknesses, in insults, in hardships, in persecutions, in difficulties. For when I am weak, then I am strong. (2 Corinthians 12:9-10)

Jesus is a living example of this passage during his temptation in the desert. Though physically weak, he was spiritually strong.

It is not a surprise that in the fourth chapter of Luke, we find Jesus tempted by Satan through the lust of the flesh, the lust of the eyes, and the pride of life. Satan is predictable in his methods and means. Jesus teaches us that the way to fight temptation is equally predictable. Let's learn from the Master.

The first thing Satan tempted Jesus with was food. In order to appeal to the **lust of the flesh** and Jesus' desire to satisfy his hunger after a long fast, Satan suggested that if Jesus really was the Son of God, he should prove it by turning the stones into bread. Just as Eve was tempted with a luscious piece of fruit, Jesus was tempted with bread. Can you imagine how tempting some freshly baked bread would be after fasting for forty days?

Jesus responded by quoting Deuteronomy 8:3, which says, *"It is written, Man does not live on bread alone, but on every word that come from the mouth of God."* Jesus quoted God's Word in order to resist this temptation. Jesus believed that God's rules were given out of God's great love for His children. Jesus put his faith in God's Word ahead of his desire to eat after a long fast. Jesus' faith in God was stronger than his need for food.

This is an example to us that when God tells us something in His Word that contradicts the lust of our flesh, we should obey God's Word, rather than our lusts. For example, you may have a natural desire to flirt with your good-looking neighbor and you even daydream about sleeping with him, even though you are married. This temptation is causing you to wane in your commitment to your husband and ignore the potential consequences of unfaithfulness. God's rules may seem like they are just in the way of you fully experiencing life and love, but if you trust that God is good and His ways are higher than your ways, you will decide to follow what God says. As you read God's Word, you see that it says that you should not commit adultery (Exodus 20:14). In order to resist temptation, you purpose to follow God, rather than your own desire, and stop thinking that having an affair is an option. Learn to rest in the truth of God's Word. Let's look at how Jesus handled the next temptation.

After this, the devil took Jesus to a high mountain and offered him the kingdoms of the earth if Jesus would bow down and worship him. This was a temptation to succumb to the **lust of the eyes.** Satan was tempting Jesus to possess something that was not his to possess at this time. Remember, the lust of the eyes deals with the sin of covetousness. If Jesus took the kingdoms of this earth under the rule of Satan, he would be coveting something that God did not want him to have at this point. Satan was now encouraging Jesus to take over the world as a leader under the authority of Satan, rather than through God's plan, which would include Jesus' death and resurrection prior to his earthly reign. As we read God's complete story, we see that Jesus will have an earthly reign at the end of the story, not in the middle of the story. The creation of Christ's Church on earth will happen as people have faith in Christ's coming kingdom "on earth as it is in heaven." Satan is trying to thwart the birth of the Church on earth with this temptation.

Jesus will one day rule the whole earth, but his earthly reign will happen after many people have been saved through his work on the cross. Jesus was full of the proper spiritual food to fight off this temptation. Fueled by his belief in God's Word, He was going to stick with God's plan. Jesus replied, *"It is written, "Worship the Lord your God, and serve him only."* (Luke 4:8 with Jesus quoting from Deuteronomy 6:13) Jesus did not fall to the temptation of taking something he wanted because it was outside of God's will. He did not fall to the temptation of possessing something that was not his to possess at that time. Jesus did not sin with the lust of the eyes.

We can learn from Jesus' example. Perhaps you are coveting what your neighbor has. You wish you had a big house or a fine car like theirs. This lust stirs in you the desire to go out and buy things you cannot afford. In order to resist this lust of the eyes, you remember that God's Word says that you should not covet (Exodus 20:17). Because you believe God's Word and are fueled by your faith, you repent of your covetous ways and stop wanting things you don't need and, perhaps, can't afford.

Finally, Satan took Jesus to the highest point of the Temple and challenged him to jump off so that angels would save him. The Devil quoted Psalm 91:11-12, *"For he will command his angels concerning you; to guard you in all your ways; they will lift you up in their hands so that you will not strike your foot against a stone."* Satan was appealing to Jesus' pride. It was with **the pride of life** that Jesus would seek glory, honor, and recognition that he was God's Son at this point. To prove that God loved him and would protect him as His one and only Son, Jesus could have jumped off of the Temple and publicly proven who he was before the proper time, but Jesus was not playing the pride game of testing God.

Eve was tempted by the devil to eat of the fruit so that she could be wise and have power like God. Eve was weak and fell to the temptation of having glory and honor like God. Jesus, on the other hand, trusted in God's timing to give him proper honor and glory as His Son.

According to the Bible, Jesus had to die on the cross and be resurrected before he was to be publicly recognized as God's Son. Jesus responded to Satan's temptation with another truth from the Bible. He quoted Deuteronomy 6:16, *"It says, do not put the Lord your God to the test."* Notice that the devil misused God's Word in order to *tempt* Christ to sin. He took the Word of God and tried to twist the meaning to put Jesus in the position of never dying on the cross for the sins of the world. If God would always guard Jesus with angels, then he would never have to die. If Jesus had interpreted God's Word this way, he would have not humbled himself and laid down his life for us. Jesus used the proper interpretation of God's Word in order to *fight* the temptation to sin. He knew that he was not to tempt and test God's love for him. Jesus would die on the cross, and yet, his required death would not mean that God had abandoned him or did not love him. Just the opposite was true. Jesus would love God like Job who in the midst of his suffering cried out, *"Though he slay me, yet will I hope in Him."* (Job 13:15)

Again, we can learn from Jesus. Perhaps you are tempted to give into the pride of life by taking credit for your natural abilities. If, for example, you have the ability to make money resulting in your being financially better off than your peers, you might feel proud that your personality is so persuasive that customers can't resist buying whatever you're selling. Your friends and family take notice and begin to praise you as some sort of god of commerce. Although your abilities and talents are a gift from God, you are tempted to give yourself credit and praise for what you have accomplished. This is a natural response, but also a sinful response. In order to avoid this temptation, you should remember that the Bible says every good gift comes from God. (James 1:17) This would cause you to be humble in your circumstances. Acting upon this truth could help you avoid giving in to the pride of life.

Jesus shows us that in order to fight the temptation of the lust of the flesh, the lust of the eyes, the pride of life, we must know God's Word, trust that His Word is true, and have the desire to obey it. As we feed our souls with God's Word, we will have the fuel to fight temptation in our lives. The Bible says, *"Submit to God, resist the devil and he will flee from you."* (James 4:7)

In your Extreme Spiritual Makeover, you can nourish your spirit and soul in the same way that Christ nourished his spirit and soul to defeat Satan and live a blameless life. You can grow wise by feeding yourself on the Word of God, each day. Remember that **each temptation is an opportunity for obedience**. Use the Word of God as fuel to fight temptation.

Be Intentional
- Use your daily Bible readings as a source for finding Bible verses and stories that will help you resist temptation.

- Connect your Bible reading time to one of your meals. This will help you to be steady in your consumption of God's Word.

- Commit to reading the One Year Bible so that you are being fed the Word of God, each day.

Questions for Personal Reflection or Group Study

- In understanding the temptation of mankind, how does J. Vernon McGee define righteousness? What does he say about character being developed in the presence of temptation? Kathy says that temptation is an opportunity for obedience. How is this true in your life?

- What are the three categories of temptation thrown at us by Satan? Define each one.

- Explain a time in your life when you were in a spiritual, emotional, or mental desert.

- How can your faith and God's Word act as fuel to help you fight temptation during these times?

Scriptures to Fuel You For the Fight: Here are attitudes that often tempt. Choose the Scriptures that can be used to fuel you to fight the temptation. Draw a line to match them up.

Temptation	Fuel To Fight
Lust	Colossians 3:9
Anger	I Timothy 3:9-10
Gossip	Romans 13:14
Lying	Colossians 3:8
Jealousy	Leviticus 19:16
	Proverbs 18:18
Envy	I Corinthians 3:3
Greed	I Timothy 3:6-7

Day Eleven
Your Personal Makeover

A Jewel of Transformation: God's Word can help you fight temptation and grow wise.

A Verse to Claim: *"How sweet are your words to taste, sweeter than honey to my mouth!"* (Psalm 119:103)

A Question to Ponder: How can I begin to fight temptation by using the truth of God's Word?

Makeover Tip to Implement: In the study questions choose one of the sins listed that is a personal temptation for you. Pick the corresponding verse chosen to fight that temptation. Record these in your makeover journal. Purpose to fight temptation by quoting God's Word, starting today.

Water - Drinking in the Holy Spirit

To him who is thirsty I will give something

to drink without cost from the spring

of the water of life.

~Revelation 21:6

Day 12
A Fluid Promise

Whoever believes in me, as the Scripture has said, will have streams of living water flow from within him.

~John 7:38

Water is the most abundant and useful substance on planet Earth. It covers more than 70 percent of the earth's surface and is part of the atmosphere above the earth. This atmosphere serves as a super highway moving water around the planet through the water cycle. The human body is approximately 55 to 75 percent water. Every system in your body needs water to function properly and to replenish itself. Depending on the temperature, human beings can only survive without water for 2 to 10 days. As your body dehydrates, your blood becomes thicker and your heart has to work harder to circulate it through your body. This is why drinking plenty of fluids is important. We need to take in between 9 and 13 cups of water every day in order to stay healthy.

God uses the symbol of life-sustaining water to describe His Holy Spirit in the Bible. *"Whoever believes in me, as the Scripture has said, will have streams of living water flow from within him."* (John 7:38)

It is God's Spirit that gives you eternal life. This Spirit, or living water, begins to flow within a believer the minute they trust Jesus as their Savior. Like water that nourishes each cell in your body and keeps the electrical signals in your nervous system firing, the Holy Spirit keeps the spirit within you alive and energized.

A Promise of Living Water

The Holy Spirit is God's fluid promise that quenches our thirst for eternal life. Jesus first introduces this concept to the woman at the well. He uses the opportunity of being thirsty and being at a well to teach about his ability to provide this "living water."

While on a journey, Jesus became thirsty and stopped in Samaria to get a drink of water. Upon seeing a local Samaritan woman at a well, he asked her for a drink. Jesus was breaking custom because the Jews from the southern portion of Judea despised the Jews from the northern area of Samaria and did not speak to them. This rift between the two groups remained because of disputes that went back centuries when the twelve tribes of Israel split into the Northern and Southern Kingdoms after Solomon's reign. Additionally, men did not normally address women in public, so the woman was shocked that Jesus spoke to her and said as much to him. Jesus replied, *"If you knew the gift of God and who it is that asks you for a drink, you would have asked him, and he would have given you living water."* (John 4:10)

The woman did not understand what Jesus was telling her, so she retorted that Jesus was implying that he thought he was better than their ancestor Jacob (Israel) who dug the very well from which they would draw water. With this, Jesus refocused the conversation, *"Everyone who drinks this water will be thirsty again, but whoever drinks the water I give him will never thirst. Indeed, the water I give him will become in him a spring of water welling up to eternal life."* (John 4:13-14)

Upon hearing this, the woman changed her tune and became interested. Jesus used this opportunity to confront her about her sinful lifestyle. He told her that he was aware that she had had five husbands and was now living with a man without being married to him. Having had her secrets revealed, the woman said that she believed Jesus must be a prophet. She added that she believed the promise that one day a Savior would come who would save people from their sinful lives and explain everything that was true to all people, even the Samaritans. *"Then Jesus declared, 'I who speak to you am he.'"* (John 4:25)

What started as a simple request for a cup of water from a local woman ended with Jesus declaring that he was the promised Savior. Wow. As the Savior, he promised this Samaritan that her faith would be rewarded with the gift of the Holy Spirit, described as "living water" that wells up in a person forever. *You* can have what Jesus promised this woman, too!

Promised Functions of the Holy Spirit

Just as water serves many functions in our bodies, the Holy Spirit serves many functions in the life of a believer. Let's review those functions.

The Holy Spirit is a Counselor, who helps you understand the ways of God. *"But the Counselor, the Holy Spirit, whom the Father will send in my name, will teach you all things and will remind you of everything I have said to you."* (John 14:26) As you study God's Word and drink in the truth about Jesus Christ, the Holy Spirit will act as a personal counselor, helping you understand the truth of what you read. The Holy Spirit will use this truth to guide you in your life decisions. This Counselor counsels free of charge.

The Holy Spirit is a Comforter to help you cope with the pain of living in a fallen world. *"I will ask the Father, and he will give you another Comforter to be with you forever—the Spirit of Truth."* (John 14:16-17) One of the benefits of having God's Spirit within you is that God can personally comfort you as you go through trials. The Holy Spirit will give you peace that surpasses understanding, even when you are experiencing terrible loss and sorrow. What an intimate and loving gift God gives to us!

The Holy Spirit is a guarantee of, or a deposit on, a future inheritance. *"The Spirit is God's guarantee that he will give us the inheritance he promised and that he has purchased us to be his own people. He did this so we would praise and glorify him."* (Ephesians 1:14) God's plan all along was to restore you to proper fellowship with Him. Your Heavenly Father gives you His Holy Spirit as a guarantee that you will receive a *physical* inheritance. This is much more than just a promise of spending eternity in heaven playing a harp and floating around on a cloud. God is promising that you will live forever in a perfect physical place in a perfect physical body. It will be a tactile experience. Wrap you mind around that, if you can!

The Holy Spirit is a cleansing agent that purifies your life by washing away sin that you have confessed and renounced. *"Christ loved the church. He gave up his life for her to make her holy and clean, washed by the cleansing of*

God's word." (Galatians 5:25-26) (NLT) With the Holy Spirit in your life, you will be empowered to put away old habits of rebellion and sin. The Holy Spirit, through God's Word, will wash away many of your desires that do not please God. This washing and transformation is a process that takes place over a lifetime of faith. Although it is not a guarantee of a sinless life, the Holy Spirit will help you develop greater obedience to God.

Having the gift of the Holy Spirit inside you forms an incredibly intimate and powerful relationship between you and God, so welcome it and allow it to transform you. The Holy Spirit teaches you God's truths and personally counsels you, developing wisdom in you. It strengthens you to fight temptation, and helps you develop godly characteristics reflecting God's image. Most importantly, the Holy Spirit enables you to live forever with Christ, making you eternal. If you have spent your whole life fearing death, fear not!

This is the living water that Jesus promised to the woman at the well, and it is living water that He promises to you, as well. Drink this beautiful promise in deeply, my friends. God is good. Cheers!

Be Intentional

- Ask the Holy Spirit to comfort you when you are going through something hard during your day.

- Ask the Holy Spirit to help you remember truth from God's Word during the day.

- Purpose to discover God's truth by relying on the Holy Spirit in you each day. Keep in mind that God's truth will never contradict what the Bible says.

- Realize that God's Spirit in you gives you the ability to forgive others today. Practice forgiving someone today.

Questions for Personal Reflection or Group Study

- How is God's Spirit like water to you spiritually?

- What was Jesus promising to give the woman at the well that he also promises to give you?

- How do the roles that the Holy Spirit plays in the life of a believer make them wise, righteous and eternal? What do you think about God transforming believers in this intimate way?

- Which aspect of the Holy Spirit do you need in your life the most?

Day Twelve
Your Personal Makeover

A Jewel of Transformation: God promised the Holy Spirit to keep your spirit alive forever.

A Verse to Claim: *"Your body is the temple of the Holy Spirit."* (I Corinthians 6:19)

A Question to Ponder: How much do I rely on the Holy Spirit each day to transform me?

Makeover Tip to Implement: Drink seven glasses of water today. Each time you drink a glass of water, pick items in which to seek God's counsel. Make this a daily internal conversation where you rely on the Holy Spirit to guide you. Write in your journal what you learn in this exercise.

Day 13

Liquid Power

I am going to send you what my Father has promised; but stay in the city until you have been clothed with power from on high.

~Luke 24:49

On the Nevada-Arizona state line sits one of the most impressive engineering accomplishments of the twentieth century, Hoover Dam. Built between 1931 and 1936, the dam produces hydroelectric power for the Southwestern United States. It uses 9.6 trillion gallons of water to produce 42 billion kilowatt hours of electricity, created when gigantic turbines capture kinetic energy from the waters of Lake Mead. This energy is funneled to generators that convert the kinetic energy into electrical energy that is sent out through a vast network of power lines to power plants that store the energy for use in homes. Over 25 million people throughout Nevada, Arizona, and California have electrical power because of the ability to capture energy from the waters that flow over Hoover Dam.

Similarly, the Holy Spirit is like living water that provides the power source for your spiritual transformation. As you tap into the Holy Spirit, you tap into God's power. It is like flipping a switch or plugging into an electrical outlet to power your transformation.

Just as Jesus promised the woman at the well that he could provide living water that would transform her spirit and soul to live forever, he promised his disciples that the Holy Spirit would serve many roles in the life of the believer. The Holy Spirit is described as a Counselor, the Spirit of Truth, a Comforter, a guarantee of an inheritance, and a Spirit that would seal them as part of God's eternal family (John 14). The Holy Spirit was the key to transforming Jesus' disciples into God's children. Jesus explained that although he would no longer be present physically, he was not abandoning them.

> *I will not leave you as orphans: I will come to you. Before long, the world will not see me anymore, but you will see me. Because I live, you also will live. On that day you will realize that I am in my Father, and you are in me, and I am in you.* (John 14:17-20)

This would be a new and very intimate relationship. It would also be a very powerful one.

Let's take a look at how Jesus fulfills this incredible promise as the disciples are gathered in the Upper Room after his resurrection and how the fulfillment of this promise transformed their lives forever.

Jesus Sends The Holy Spirit

From its first appearance, we can see the amazing transformative impact of the Holy Spirit. In the first chapter of Acts, Jesus, after his resurrection, gave some final instructions to his disciples before ascending into heaven, *"Do not leave Jerusalem, but wait for the gift which my Father promised, which you have heard me speak about. For John baptized with water, but in a few days you will be baptized by the Holy Spirit."* (Acts 1:4)

The word "baptized" up to this point in the Scriptures was associated with being completely immersed, covered, and washed clean by water. Jesus used this word to describe how the Holy Spirit would function in the disciples' lives. It would immerse, cover, and purify them. This cleansing would be as though by fire and they would never need to be cleansed again. The disciples could not have fully anticipated the nature of this "baptism," but they didn't have to wait long to find out.

Fifty days after Jesus' death and resurrection, the disciples were together in the Upper Room when a sound like the blowing of a violent wind came from heaven and filled the whole house. Something that looked like tongues of fire rested on their shoulders, causing them to speak in foreign languages that they had not previously known.

At this time, many Jews from foreign lands who spoke these languages were in Jerusalem to celebrate Pentecost (a religious Jewish festival). When the crowds heard the roaring wind, they went to the house where the disciples were gathered to see what was happening. Upon arriving, they were amazed to hear the disciples testifying about the truth of God in their own languages.

When some of them accused the disciples of being drunk, Peter addressed the crowd to explain what was happening, *"These men are not drunk, as you suppose. It's only nine in the morning! No, this is what was spoken by the prophet Joel."* (Acts 2:15-16) Joel had prophesied that one day, God would pour out His Spirit upon His people and whoever called upon the name of the Lord would be saved. (Joel 2) Peter, who was an uneducated fisherman, gave an impassioned sermon worthy of the greatest theologian, concluding with a clear explanation of Jesus' identity. *"Therefore let all Israel be assured of this: God has made this Jesus, whom you crucified, both Lord and Christ."* (Acts 2:36) This was the same Peter who had vehemently denied that he even knew Jesus on the eve of his crucifixion. Now, with the Holy Spirit dwelling within him, Peter boldly proclaims Christ as the risen Lord and Savior. Peter's words, empowered by the Holy Spirit, touched the hearts of many and over three thousand people came to believe in Jesus as the Christ that day.

The Holy Spirit transformed Peter's life. The fruit of the Holy Spirit was immediately seen as Peter boldly shared the truth about Christ with love, joy, and peace. Peter is not the only disciple whose life reflected transformation after receiving the Holy Spirit. The disciples were initially a motley crew, reflecting little faith in God and given over to pettiness, competitiveness, and pride when Jesus first chose them. Almost completely without religious training, the disciples were simple men with simple faith that lacked depth and conviction. Christian tradition teaches that after receiving the Holy Spirit, these same men spread the truth of God's Word across the known world, teaching the deep truths of the Bible to the masses with bold faith and extraordinary knowledge. **The Holy Spirit transformed them into pillars of faith, most of whom gave up their own lives in defense of the gospel.** Their transformations reflect the power of God's Spirit in them.

This same power is available to you and will be seen in the fruit your life produces.

The Fruit of the Spirit

We started this day by establishing that the Holy Spirit is the power within you that can transform you to reflect the image of God. It is important to realize that you must *choose* to tap into this power that is available within you. This means that you must intentionally rely on God, rather than yourself, to accomplish the small tasks you face each day, as well as to conquer the large problems that life presents.

Just as you can tell when an apple tree is healthy and growing because of the fruit it produces, when the Holy Spirit flows through your life, it will produce certain godly qualities in your personality. *"But the fruit of the Spirit is love, joy, peace, patience, kindness, goodness, faithfulness, gentleness and self-control."* (Galatians 5:22-23) We discussed on Day One how true beauty is seen in our attitudes and our actions. God graciously gives us the fruit of the Holy Spirit so that we can be transformed with beautiful attitudes. So how do we develop these character qualities?

In John 15:5, Jesus describes how this works, *"Yes, I am the vine; you are the branches. Those who remain in me, and I in them, will produce much fruit. For apart from me you can do nothing."* (NLT) In order for these qualities to bloom inside of you, you must be positioned as a branch on the vine. It is the branch's connection to the vine that enables it to be fed and nourished by the sap of the plant. If the branch is properly attached, it will receive the sap, be nourished, and produce clusters of grapes. In the same way, you (the branch) will produce love, joy, peace, patience, kindness, goodness, faithfulness, gentleness, and self-control (the fruit) in your life if you are attached to Jesus (the Vine) and allow the Holy Spirit (the sap) to flow through you and nourish you.

The fruit of the Spirit is not something you have to try to produce in your life, because it is a natural result of being in Christ. **You will produce more fruit, though, as you trust**

Christ more deeply with every aspect of your life.

The power of God's Spirit is what gives you the ability to transform from an ugly duckling into beautiful swan. You were made for this very purpose and as you rely on the Holy Spirit, you will develop the kind of beauty that God intended. This is the kind of beauty that will last forever. Let your dependence upon God result in beautiful attitudes seen in the fruit of the Spirit in your life.

God also provides by giving gifts to his children that enable beautiful actions, as well as beautiful attitudes.

The Spiritual Gifts

The power of the Holy Spirit is what transforms your personality to be like God's by its influence on your attitudes and actions. We discussed how your attitudes will change as you use the sap of the Holy Spirit to produce the fruit of the Spirit in your personality. Now, we see that God's plan is also to transform your actions by gifting you in certain areas so that you can be His *body* on earth to accomplish His *will* on earth. His will on earth was stated in the Great Commission in Matthew 28:19-20, *"Therefore go and make disciples of all the nations, baptizing them in the name of the Father and the Son and the Holy Spirit and teaching them to obey everything that I commanded you."* **The spiritual gifts are the tools given by God to help believers accomplish the mission of the Church on earth.** As you open your gifts from God and begin to share them with others, your testimony about Christ extends to people who did not previously know Him, encourages believers in their faith, and comforts those going through trials. 1 Peter 4:10 explains, *"Each one should use whatever gift he has received to serve others, faithfully administering God's grace in its various forms."*

One reason that your Extreme Spiritual Makeover is so important is that God wants to use *you* to help establish and build His kingdom. He has given you specific gifts and talents so that you can spread His grace to others. By using your gifts, more people can come to know God. This is why it is so important for you to transform into the beautiful person He created you to be. The gifts of the Holy Spirit are keys to this process.

There are over twenty gifts listed in Scripture that are given to individual believers to be used within Christ's Church so that the many members of his body will function as a single cohesive unit. Romans 12:4-6 says, *"Just as each of us has one body with many members, and these members do not all have the same function, so in Christ we who are many form one body, and each member belongs to all the others. We have different gifts, according to the grace given us."*

No individual believer is given all of the gifts, but each believer is given more than one of the gifts to benefit others. These gifts will become evident as you get involved in ministries and work in your local church and community. As you mature in your faith, some gifts will appear that were not evident early in your journey. Many times, your friends and family will be able to see your areas of gifting better than you can because they will be the beneficiaries of your gifts and talents. So, what are these gifts from God? The gifts are listed in different parts of the Bible including Romans 12, 1 Corinthians 12, and Ephesians 4, as well as many other passages. Let's take a look at some of the gifts:

- **Prophecy-** (Romans 12:6) The ability to unabashedly share truth from Scripture.

- **Service** also called **Helps-** (Romans 12:7) The ability to meet the needs of others by doing necessary tasks.

- **Teaching-** (Romans 12:7) The ability to understand the Word of God, clearly explain it to others, and apply it.

- **Encouragement-** (Romans 12:8) The ability to bless others through one's words and actions.

- **Giving-** (Romans 12:8) The ability to contribute money and resources in the Church with joy and generosity.

- **Leadership** also called **Administration-** (Romans 12:8) The ability to influence others with directions and specific goals, bringing order out of chaos.

- **Mercy-** (Romans 12:8) The demonstration of genuine sensitivity to suffering. The ability to really "be there" for people who are in need.

- **Wisdom-** (1 Corinthians 12:8) The ability to effectively apply God's Word to meet a specific need in a specific situation.

- **Knowledge-** (1 Corinthians 12:8) The ability to bring truth to other believers through a revelation or Biblical insight.

- **Faith-** (1 Corinthians 12:9) The ability to unwaveringly trust God in the most adverse circumstances.

- **Healing-** (1 Corinthians 12:9) The ability to restore people to emotional, relational, spiritual, or physical wholeness.

- **Miracles-** (1 Corinthians 12:10) The ability to authenticate the message and work of God through supernatural interventions that point to Him.

- **Discernment-** (1 Corinthians 12:10) The unusual ability to see through confusion, identify the problem, and reveal the solution. Sometimes this includes identifying the presence of evil. The ability to give wise counsel.

- **Tongues-** (1 Corinthians 12:10) The ability from God to speak, to worship, or pray in a language not previously known to the speaker.

- **Interpretation of Tongues**- (1 Corinthians 12:10) The ability to understand and explain to other believers what is being spoken when a person who has the gift of tongues is speaking in a foreign language. This is necessary for edifying anyone who is hearing the message of God.

- **Apostleship**- (Ephesians 4:11) The ability to start and oversee the development of new churches or ministries.

- **Evangelism**- (Ephesians 4:11) The ability to communicate the story of Jesus effectively and clearly to those who do not yet know him.

- **Pastoring** or **Shepherding**- (Ephesians 4:11) The ability to lead and nurture others as they grow in their faith.

- **Hospitality**- (1 Peter 4:9-10) The ability to create a warm, welcoming environment where people feel valued, loved, and cared for.

- **Intercession**- (1 Timothy 2:1-2) The ability to faithfully pray on behalf of other people and see frequent and specific results.

- **Craftsmanship** - (Exodus 28; Acts 9:39) The ability to creatively design or construct items for ministry.

These gifts, given by God to His children, are to be used within the body of Christ to spread the Good News about God's desire to be reconciled with His creation through Jesus Christ. They enable you to participate in the mission of telling the world about God. Please remember that God wants to use your whole personality and all of your abilities and talents to draw others to the truth about God and the fact that He is our loving Creator.

Think about these gifts and which descriptions fit your abilities and tendencies. God wants to transform you for His glory and using your spiritual gifts is part of this process. The Holy Spirit, which is the power of God in you, will make your gifts evident as you follow your interests and passions in serving others. The beautiful truth is that He designed your personality, passions, and gifts to match the needs of other people. So get busy serving others and your God-given gifts will emerge!

Be Intentional

- List gifts from the spiritual gifts list given that fit your personality, talents, and tendencies.

- Consider ways to use your gifts to help others in your church, community, and family.

- Purpose to start serving others with your natural abilities and God's supernatural gifts given to you. Unwrap His gifts and share them.

Questions for Personal Reflection or Group Discussion

- How is the Holy Spirit like stored electricity or untapped sap in a grape vine?

- How was this power evidenced in Peter when Jesus first sent the Holy Spirit to the disciples?

- What are the fruits of the Spirit and how can you grow this fruit in your life?

- Why does God give people certain spiritual gifts in their personality and how can you begin to identify and unwrap the gifts He has given to you?

- Why is these gifts designed to be shared and not hoarded?

- Discuss why this liquid power makes you more beautiful like Christ?

Day Thirteen
Your Personal Makeover

A Jewel of Transformation: God sent His Holy Spirit to power your transformation.

A Verse to Claim: *"But when he, the Spirit of truth, comes, he will guide you into all truth."* (John 16:13)

A Question to Ponder: In what ways is my life reflecting the growth of the fruit of the Spirit in me?

Makeover Tip to Implement: In order to develop love and patience, purpose to sit down to listen to a friend who needs to talk. Do not talk about yourself during this time. Only listen to details about their life. Record in your ESM journal how you felt during the conversation. Think about hard times in your life. List the fruit of the Spirit that you grew in your life at that time. Write in your journal about your experience.

Prayer - Getting Your Daily Sunshine

Sunshine on my shoulders makes me happy.
Sunshine in my eyes can make me cry.
Sunshine on the water looks so lovely.
Sunshine almost always makes me high.
~John Denver

Day 14

Walking On Sunshine

If we genuinely love people,

we desire for them more than is

within our power to give,

and that will cause us to pray.

~Richard Foster

How much time do you spend in direct sun light each day? Recent reports on the dangers of UVA and UVB rays from the sun have caused many people to always protect their skin with sunscreen or avoid even going into direct sunlight altogether. While staying out of the sun to prevent skin cancer and premature aging might initially seem like a good idea, studies show that some exposure to direct sunlight on the skin is very important to our health. The sun's rays on the skin produce a vitamin in our bodies called vitamin D3. Known as the "sunshine vitamin," vitamin D3 is one of the most useful nutritional tools we have. Studies have shown that this vitamin is linked to a reduction in the occurrence of depression, the prevention of bone loss, increased mental concentration, improved immune system, and even cancer prevention. Amazingly, the sun's rays start a chemical reaction in our bodies that creates this vital vitamin.

As an Extreme Spiritual Makeover candidate there is a type of spiritual sunshine that you must get each day: prayer. **Prayer provides the communication with God that energizes your soul to become more like Christ's.** Prayer is like sunshine to your soul because prayer prevents depression, improves your spiritual health, and starts a spiritual reaction that prompts God to respond to you. Prayer is powerful.

Prayer Matters

When I was young in my Christian faith, I can remember wondering if anyone was really listening when I prayed. Sometimes, I felt like I was wishing on a star for things to be different in my life. I lacked confidence in my relationship with God and was not sure that prayer "worked." I questioned whether God was really listening to me.

Over the years, the doubts of my younger years have been replaced with the confidence that God does, indeed, hear my prayers and answers them as His will allows. God's subtle and sometimes not so subtle responses to my cries for help, my whines of discomfort, and my honest questions of faith have bolstered my relationship with Him. Like the sunshine of dawn that bursts through the darkness of night, prayer has helped me to see the truth in God's Word. God has a purpose for all of mankind as His story unfolds and prayer plays a part in how you can begin to understand God's story. As you read the Bible and think about what it has to say, prayer is one way to process what you are reading. Talk to God about the concepts, stories, and principles that are in this sacred book. If you have questions, prayer is the vehicle for asking them. **God hears you and will answer you through circumstances in your life, through the lessons in the Bible, and through the wisdom of other believers.**

Prayer can be a stabilizing force in your life. Prayer can help you realize that even though you may waver in your belief, God is faithful. If you sometimes feel emotionally absent in your relationship with God, He is present and available. You may be apathetic, but God is interested. Perhaps you feel distant from Him, but God seeks to be close to you. One of the keys to fostering intimacy with God and developing His image in you is to pray. *"And pray in the Spirit on all occasions with all kinds of prayers and requests. With this in mind, be alert and always keep on praying for all the saints."* (Ephesians 6:18) God longs to be in fellowship with you. You were created for this very purpose. This is why prayer is so important.

Daniel – An Example in Prayer

When you want to learn how to do something, you find an expert or someone with a great deal of experience who can teach you. Prayer is no exception. In order to learn how to pray effectively, it behooves you to consult a "prayer expert." The Bible gives us such an expert in Daniel, a renowned prayer warrior. Daniel was a man who was incredibly disciplined in his faith, and particularly disciplined in the practice of daily prayer. It was his incredible commitment to prayer that got him thrown into the lions' den.

Daniel's life was not easy. As a teenager he was carted off to a foreign land as part of the Babylonian captivity of the Jews. In spite of this, Daniel maintained his faith in God and his obedience to God's laws, praying daily, even in this Gentile nation. Because of his character and superior intelligence, Daniel rose from being a lowly captive to a royal administrator, second only to the king in both the Babylonian and Persian Empires.

Despite his high rank in a Gentile government, Daniel continued the discipline of praying to the God of Israel each day. Envious underlings sought to undermine Daniel's favored position and tricked the King into signing a law prohibiting anyone from praying to anyone other than the King. Daniel, of course, opted to continue his daily prayer ritual, choosing God's law over man's law, so his enemies had him thrown into the lions' den. God rescued Daniel by shutting the mouths of the hungry lions as Daniel stood in their midst all night. In the morning, when he found that Daniel was still alive, King Darius declared his belief in Daniel's God and sent a letter of testimony about God's greatness to his entire kingdom.

Daniel lived an amazing life committed to God. His experience in the lions' den, which is in the sixth chapter of the book of Daniel, is but one of the many fascinating stories of his faithfulness to God and God's faithfulness to him. It would be well worth your time to read the book of Daniel to learn more about the life of this hero of the faith, including how to pray.

How To Pray

Since Daniel is our prayer expert, let's take a look at how Daniel prayed. There is a method to effective prayer. Daniel does four things in his prayer to God in Daniel 9:4-19 that are important for each of us to do as we pray each day:

- **A**dore God.

- **C**onfess to God.

- **T**hank God.

- **S**upplications requested of God.

Some people call this the "ACTS" method of prayer. In Daniel 9:4, we read, *"O Lord, the great and awesome God, who keeps his covenant of love with all who love him and obey his commands...."* This is an **adoration** of who God is. You should begin your prayers in this way.

Daniel 4:5-6 continues, *"...we have sinned and done wrong. We have been wicked and have rebelled; we have turned away from your commands and laws. We have not listened to your servants and prophets who spoke to our kings, our princes, and our fathers, and to all the people of the land."* This is **confession** of sin, which is important when approaching our Holy God. Remember to confess your sins to God.

In Daniel 4:15 and 16, Daniel begins each sentence, *"O Lord our God, who brought your people out of Egypt with a mighty hand and who made for yourself a name that endures to this very day..."* and *"O Lord, in keeping with all your righteous acts...."* These are prayers of **thanksgiving** that Daniel showers upon God for all that He has done for His people. Remember to thank God for what He has done in your life each day.

Finally, in Daniel 4:17-19, Daniel asks God to provide for the needs of the Israelites, *"O Lord, look with favor on your desolate sanctuary. Give ear, O God, and hear; open your eyes and see the desolation....O Lord, listen! O Lord, forgive! O Lord, hear and act! For your sake, O my God, do not delay, because your city and your people bear your Name."* This is where Daniel is asking God to answer specific needs. This is **supplication**. You must ask God each day to act on your behalf and on behalf of those you love. Entreat Him to fulfill His promises on earth and to do His will in the lives of His children.

Daniel shows us that adoration, humble confession, cheerful thanksgiving, and earnest supplication will open the pathways of communication with your Creator. You can pray these same types of prayer to God.

Do you want to know God? Begin to approach Him in prayer like Daniel. This is how you will develop intimacy with your Creator.

Jesus Teaches About Prayer

Pray continually.
~I Thessalonians 5:17

Now, we have the opportunity to learn about prayer from God, Himself. **Jesus is our greatest example of how to achieve intimacy with God through prayer.** It is no wonder that after watching his ability to have a constant dialogue with his Father in heaven and then control his attitudes and actions with perfection, Jesus' disciples pestered him to teach them how to pray. They wanted to know his secrets. How and why did his prayer life result in such beauty and perfection?

Jesus teaches his disciples how to pray by giving them the Lord's Prayer as an example,

> *After this manner, therefore pray ye: Our Father which art in heaven, Hallowed be thy name. Thy kingdom come, Thy will be done in earth, as it is in heaven. Give us this day our daily bread. And forgive us our debts, as we forgive our debtors. And lead us not into temptation, but deliver us from evil: For thine is the kingdom, and the power, and the glory, forever. Amen.* (Matthew 6:9-13) (KJV)

Notice that Jesus closely follows the ACTS pattern of prayer. Here are some keys to talking to God based on the Lord's Prayer:

- Jesus encourages us to call God our Father. Doing this acknowledges our position as God's children. It also implies that God is the One who created us, provides for us, and will give us an inheritance. Jesus uses the word Abba or "daddy." There is a familiarity and intimacy in addressing Him. We are to feel close to God like we would with our own daddy, knowing that He loves us and wants to take care of us.

- We are to praise God for who He is and the holiness of His name. This is **adoration**.

- We are to ask God to bring about His Kingdom on earth. This is an important part of God's story. God intends to restore paradise on this earth. We are to pray for this to occur, just as Daniel did.

- God wants us to ask for the provision of our daily bread. This "daily bread" is representative of our daily needs, both physical and spiritual. Remember that Christ is our manna from heaven. It is Christ who sustains us physically and spiritually.

- We are to ask that our sins be forgiven. This is **confession.** We must confess our sins and request forgiveness. This is a powerful and important part of becoming beautiful. This is exfoliating sin.

- We are to acknowledge that we are forgiving those who sin against us, just as we are forgiven by God. Remember that our grateful response for God so graciously forgiving us is to turn around and forgive others who have sinned against us.

- We are to ask God to protect us from the temptations of Satan. Remember that we can rely on the truth of God's Word to resist temptation. Only God can protect us from evil. This is **supplication.**

- When we state that His is the kingdom, power, and glory, forever, we are being thankful for the truth about God and what He accomplishes. This is **thanksgiving.**

- Jesus reminds us to be persistent in our **supplication**.

We are to ask, seek, and knock. He explains this in Luke 11:9, *"So I say to you: Ask and it will be given to you; seek and you will find; knock and the door will be opened to you."* If we pray persistently in the way that He teaches through the Lord's prayer, God will say "yes" to our requests to fulfill His will on earth, help us to find the Truth, and open the door to heaven for us. We are to always pray for *His* will, not *ours*. These words do not mean that whatever you ask in Christ's name, you will receive. There is false teaching that promotes this idea. The stipulation for an affirmative answer from God in prayer is that you are seeking God's will for that situation. God will always answer, "yes" if you are asking that His will be done. God will cause His will to prevail on earth and in Heaven.

Improve your inner beauty by getting your daily dose of spiritual sunshine. Start the spiritual process of interacting with God by talking to him in prayer.

Be Intentional

- Start a personal prayer journal.
- Practice the ACTS method of prayer.
- Pick one of the psalms in the Bible and try to pray that psalm out loud to God.
- See if you can make that psalm your personal

prayer to God and your adoration of God in prayer.

- Record things that you need to confess to God in your journal.

- Record things that you want to thank God for in your journal.

- Record things that you need to ask God to help you with in your life and the lives of your family and friends.

Questions for Personal Reflection or Group Study

- On a scale of 1 to 10 how much prayer/spiritual sunshine do you get each day?

- How does prayer play a part in this statement, "God longs to be in fellowship with you."

- What does ACTS stand for?

- Why is talking and communicating important in any relationship?

- How can you develop some of the intimacy with God that both Daniel and Jesus had?

Day Fourteen
Your Personal Makeover

A Jewel of Transformation: The communication with God accomplished through prayer energizes you to become more beautiful like Christ.

A Verse to Claim: *"Pray continually."* (I Thessalonians 5:17)

A Question to Ponder: What types of things do I pray about when I pray?

Makeover Tip to Implement: Begin a new prayer list in your journal. Follow the pattern of the Lord's Prayer that Jesus taught and Daniel practiced. Take note of the difference in the length of your prayer time.

Day 15
Energy from Prayer

Prayer is where the action is.

~John Wesley

My God, I pretend to nothing upon this earth, except to be so firmly united to you by prayer that to be separated from you may be impossible; let others desire riches and glory; for my part, I desire but one thing, and that is, to be inseparably united to you, and to place in you alone all my hopes of happiness and repose.

~St. John Climacus

We learned yesterday that intimacy with God is developed through prayer. The anatomy of prayer includes adoration of God, confession of our sins, thanksgiving for His blessings, and supplication or asking for our needs to be met. Practicing this form of communication is like spiritual sunshine to your soul.

We have discussed that one of God's purposes in creating you is to have a deep and abiding relationship with you. God is relational and wants intimacy. Prayer is a tool for developing that intimacy between you and God, but like most things, you will only get out of it what you put into it. One of the keys to a good prayer life is truly opening up to God. It is important to express your raw emotions and deepest feelings to Him.

Your relationship with God is not unlike your relationship with anyone else you love. There are certain things that are required for the relationship to work.

- First, you must know the person well.

- Second, you must trust the person to be faithful to you, and you must be faithful to them.

- Third, you must maintain steady communication in order to keep the relationship alive.

- Fourth, you must pour yourself into the relationship by being vulnerable and honest with the one you love.

By spending time together, listening to each other, and trusting each other, the strong bond of love will last. This is exactly what needs to occur in your relationship with God.

God describes His relationship with believers as that of

a marriage relationship (Ephesians 5). Within a marriage, communication and trust are keys to success. Just as a husband and wife must communicate openly in order to develop love, you need to pray honestly, fully exposing yourself to God in order to develop intimacy with Him.

As you read the Bible and pray daily, you will come to know Him and trust that He loves you. It is then that as He answers your prayers, whether those answers are what you originally hoped for, you will take those answers as loving responses to your needs. You will find strength and hope through your relationship with God, if you pour all of yourself into your relationship with Him, coming to know all of who He is.

With this in mind, it is important in your Extreme Spiritual Makeover to practice pouring your heart out to God in prayer. The warmth of God's love experienced as you pray is the sunshine your soul craves. It is at our weakest times that the energy from God, found through communicating with Him in prayer, strengthens us to endure trials. The Bible shows us one woman who found hope through prayer. Her name was Hannah.

The Faithful Pray

The story of Hannah in the book of I Samuel is one of the best-loved stories of answered prayer in the Bible. Hannah was an example of someone who had a deep, personal relationship with God. She was a woman who trusted God with the longings of her heart and was not afraid to approach Him to reveal her pain and ask Him to relieve her suffering. Hers was a story of sorrow, suffering, petition, and victory through prayer.

Hannah endured one of the hardest things any woman can face - infertility. Unable to bear a child, Hannah was further humiliated by her husband's other wife, who was able to have children. *"And because the Lord had closed her womb, her rival kept provoking her in order to irritate her."* (I Samuel 1:6) Year after year, Hannah endured the pain of not being able to bear a child, compounded by the burden of being harassed by her rival. Any woman who has struggled with fertility issues knows the heartache of an empty womb. Hannah was a woman of faith, so rather than being bitter and angry with God, she was simply sad. Her response to her circumstances was a sign of her humility.

The years went by with no change. Finally, on one of their trips to worship at the Temple, Hannah wept bitterly at the Temple doorpost and poured out her heart to God in prayer. She promised God that if He would grant her a child, she would dedicate her son to the Lord's service. Eli, the High Priest at the Temple, watched Hannah's dramatic prayer session. Her lips moved furiously, but her voice was silent. Eli thought she was drunk and promptly told her to get rid of her wine. Hannah corrected him and explained her plight. *"Do not take your servant for a wicked woman; I have been praying here out of my great anguish and grief."* (1 Samuel 1:16) Eli answered that he hoped the God of Israel would grant her what she had asked of him. Here, we see that in communicating with God, Hannah truly opened herself up to His will.

After praying, Hannah's soul was revived. *"Then she went her way and ate something, and her face was no longer downcast."* (I Samuel 1:18) Being able to pour out her anguish to God in prayer was like sunshine to Hannah's soul. Light entered her dark place. God heard Hannah's prayer, and she became pregnant with a son. *"I prayed for this child and the Lord has heard my prayer."* (I Samuel 1:27) Hannah named her son Samuel.

After young Samuel was weaned, but while he was still quite young, Hannah honored her promise to the Lord and took Samuel to live in service to God at the Temple. *"So now I give him to the Lord. For his whole life he will be given over to the Lord."* (I Samuel 1:18) There was tremendous strength and resolve in what Hannah did here. Can you imagine the courage and faith it would take to give up your firstborn son? She was able to surrender Samuel to God because of her complete trust in Him. Hannah knew that God loved her and that His purposes for her life and for the life of her son were good.

In 1 Samuel 2, we see the beautiful prayer of Hannah upon delivering her only son to the Temple to begin his lifetime of service to God. It is a prayer of joy and praise. *"My heart rejoices in the Lord; in the Lord my horn is lifted high. My mouth boasts over my enemies, for I delight in your deliverance."* (1 Samuel 2:1) Indeed, through prayer, Hannah went from the dark shadow of infertility to the bright sunshine of giving birth to her first son and dedicating him to God. She overcame her enemy through the strength of the Lord. This was a woman who knew God intimately. This was a believer who trusted in God's will on earth. She understood that she was part of God's bigger story and she humbly played her part. We can learn much from this beautiful soul.

Do you bare your soul to God in prayer? Could you ever be accused of being drunk in prayer because of your honest, emotional cries to God?

Jesus Finds Strength In Prayer

Jesus is another example of a person who relied on prayer to find strength in a difficult situation. Jesus also poured out his heart to his Father as he contemplated his future suffering and death on the cross. Does it surprise you that the Savior of the world would have one of the most gripping and difficult prayer sessions in the Bible? In his frail human body, Christ had to rely on the power of prayer to find strength and resolve for his life's purpose. Luke 22 and Matthew 26 give two accounts of Jesus' prayers in the Garden of Gethsemane.

Jesus Prays Through Pain

In Luke's account, we learn from Jesus that prayer is the best tool for dealing with anxiety, stress, and anguish. We studied how Jesus faced his truth through prayer on Day Nine. Jesus taught us to not run from our pain, but be willing to feel it and deal with it. He did not avoid his sorrow by drinking wine or taking drugs. He faced his trials with humility. *"And being in anguish, he prayed more earnestly, and his sweat was like great drops of blood falling to the ground."* (Luke 22:44)

Jesus was present in his pain. That did not make the situation easy. Jesus was in anguish over the prospect of carrying the weight of the world's sins upon him. He dreaded the looming separation from His Father that would occur as he hung on the cross, and his sorrow and anxiety were so great his sweat was like great drops of blood. Talk about stress!

Prayer is a key tool for living *your* truth. What great sorrow do you have in your life? What pain do you need to be present for? Prayer is the way for you to handle your truth, whatever it may be. Prayer brought Jesus to the point of acceptance as he prepared to be the sacrifice for many. Prayer can bring you to a point of acceptance and surrender, too.

Jesus Prays Alone

In Matthew's account, we see the overwhelming stress and grief that Jesus had as he contemplated being separated from His Father by our sins. Jesus expressed his despair to Peter, James, and John, *"My soul is overwhelmed with sorrow to the point of death."* (Matthew 26:38) He asked them to stay with him in this trial and pray. In anguish, he fell down to the ground and asked God to take this cup from him, if it was God's will. He returned to find the disciples asleep, rather than praying. Oh, how true this account rings! Have you ever felt alone in your pain?

Once again, Jesus went to a private place and prayed about his pending death and separation from God. He wanted to avoid this if there was any other way to accomplish salvation, but he wanted God's will, not his own. *"My Father, if it is not possible for this cup to be taken away unless I drink it, may your will be done."* (Matthew 26:42) Do you sense that Jesus' vulnerability and how he had to rely on the strength of the Spirit to overcome physical weakness? The disciples were not strong enough to overcome their weak bodies, and Jesus found them asleep, rather than praying for him.

Jesus prayed once more. The third time was a charm. After this prayer session, we see a steely resolve in Christ. He was prepared for his fate. He was not a victim of his fate. He was living his truth, having chosen to follow God's will. He was the victor who was willing to face death and overcome the world. With the power of prayer, he became the person who willingly gave his life for the world. What a hero we have in Jesus Christ!

What have you found the courage to face through prayer? How has prayer energized you?

Application

We saw in the books of 1 Samuel, Luke, and Matthew that God is aware of our problems. He desires to communicate with us and help us through those problems. Hannah received a "yes" to her prayers for a child, but Jesus received a "no" when he asked that the cup pass from him. God loved both Hannah and Jesus, but gave two different answers to their heart-felt prayers.

Both Hannah and Jesus came to God with deep sorrows and specific requests. Their complete trust in God enabled them to honestly lay out the passionate desires of their hearts to Him. God met each of them at their point of need. He answered when they called, and both Hannah and Jesus drew immediate strength and comfort from prayer. Hannah was encouraged to face what life would bring to her, while Jesus was encouraged to face what death would mean for him. Prayer revitalized their spiritual lives.

You must develop your relationship with God through daily prayer. Daily communication with God about the problems in your life, both big and small, will improve your attitude and give you renewed hope for God's loving purpose in your life. You will be energized by His love and this will make you a more beautiful person.

Be Intentional

- Continue using your personal prayer journal.
- Record your struggles, prayer requests, and God's answers to you.
- Did you get a "yes" or a "no" from God? Maybe you received a "wait."
- Record how you felt about God's answers or silence.
- Try to pray for your governmental officials and your nation, as well as your family and friends, each day.
- Pray for someone who is being persecuted for his or her faith.

Questions for Personal Reflection or Group Discussion

- What do you think John Wesley meant when he said, "Prayer is where the action is?"

- What did you learn about prayer from reading both Hannah's and Jesus' stories?

- How were each of them more spiritually beautiful because of their practice of praying to God?

- Explain what you have learned about praying for God's will rather than your own will.

Day Fifteen
Your Personal Makeover

A Jewel of Transformation: Prayer cultivates your intimacy with God and helps you accept God's will, even in suffering.

A Verse to Claim: *"Do not be anxious for anything, but by prayer and petition, with thanks, let your requests be known to God."* (Philippians 4:6)

A Question to Ponder: Am I willing to pray for God's will in my life, rather than my own will?

Makeover Tip to Implement: Write a prayer for yourself and your family in your ESM journal. Read it aloud to your family. Remember to include true statements about God in the prayer. Remember to include that you want His will to be done.

Exercise - Walking the Walk And Weight Lifting

There is no exercise better for the heart than reaching down and lifting people up.
~John Andrew Holmes

Day 16
Doing Cardio God's Way

And let us consider how we may spur one another on toward love and good deeds.

~Hebrews 10:24

No physical makeover is complete without a regular exercise program. Cardiovascular health and emotional well-being are tied to physical exertion. Health experts agree that thirty minutes of aerobic exercise daily provides numerous health benefits. Aerobic exercise increases the heart rate and oxygen level in the blood. This is important because oxygen is the key element in the process of respiration. Respiration uses oxygen to convert calories from the food we eat into energy for our body's use. Daily exercise not only increases blood circulation and muscle tone, it also helps keep our weight under control by enabling the process of converting food into energy.

Similarly, a healthy Christian life is not possible without daily exercise. Walking the Christian walk is tied to the well being of the soul. The Bible says, *"As the body without the spirit is dead, so faith without deeds is dead."* (James 2:26) So, then, our faith is exercised and kept alive by love and good deeds.

As an Extreme Spiritual Makeover candidate, you should be nourished by God's Word. It is the daily intake of God's Word that gives you the spiritual calories and energy you need to love others. It is what powers you to do cardio God's way. If you read the Bible daily, but never do any good works or loving acts for others, it is like eating too many calories and not burning them off with exercise. Just as not exercising leads to being overweight, not doing good works leads to being spiritually unhealthy.

How is your cardiovascular health when it comes to doing good works and having loving attitudes towards others? Are you a spiritual couch potato or a marathon runner? Would your family and friends describe you as a spiritual athlete who is in great shape or a benchwarmer who never gets in the game?

Exercising By Loving Your Neighbor

And do not forget to do good and to share with others,
for with such sacrifices is God pleased.

(Hebrews 13:16)

God calls us to exercise by walking the walk and not just talking the talk. By loving others outside of our circle of family and friends, we learn to love the way God loves. The story of the Good Samaritan is a great example of how to love your neighbor. Jesus tells this parable while he is teaching a group scholars and teachers. One of the teachers of the Law inquired how a person might obtain eternal life. Jesus asked him how he interpreted God's Law. The teacher answered, *"'Love the Lord with all your heart and all of your soul and with all your strength and with all your mind,' and, 'Love your neighbor as yourself.'"* (Luke 10:27) Jesus responded that if he was able to do this, he would live forever.

Being a teacher of the law, the man wanted Jesus to be more specific about exactly whom he must love. He wanted to know, "Who is my neighbor?" Jesus answered with a parable. This story of the Good Samaritan explains the extent of the obligation we have to love others. You know the story.

There was a Jewish man traveling from Jerusalem to Jericho who was accosted by robbers, beat up, stripped down, and left for dead by the side of the road. A short time later, a priest came down the road, saw the injured man, but passed by on the other side of the road without helping him. Then, a Levite (a man who serves in the Temple in Jerusalem and was part of the religious class) came along, saw him and also passed him by. Finally, a Samaritan came along, saw the man, and felt compassion for him. He stopped, bandaged the man's wounds, put him on his own donkey, and took him to an inn where he cared for him. The next day before continuing on his journey, the Samaritan made arrangements for the innkeeper to care for the man. The Samaritan even paid for all of the man's expenses until he recovered.

After relaying this story, Jesus asked the teacher of the Law, *"Which of these three do you think proved to be a neighbor to the man who fell into the robbers' hands?"* (Luke 10:36) The teacher acknowledged that it was the one who showed mercy towards the man. Having established the extent of our obligation to love others, Jesus told the teacher, *"Go and do likewise."* (Luke 10:37)

But Jesus had an even stronger lesson in this parable. It is not just that the robbery victim was a stranger to the Good Samaritan. The magnitude of the lesson is that the Jewish victim would have been an *enemy* of the Samaritan. This Samaritan's love for his *enemy* resulted in a godly example of exercising one's spiritual muscles by loving your neighbor, even if they may be a cultural enemy. *That* is the love of God lived out in a life of faith! Jesus requires this kind of love from you and me.

Exercising By Loving Your Enemies

If the Extreme Spiritual Makeover candidate wants to get into excellent spiritual shape, it is not enough to just love your neighbors. To get in really good shape you must practice loving your enemies. Yes, I am talking about forgiving those who have hurt you and blessing those who curse you. **The most beautiful people, who are truly eternally beautiful, have mastered the art of loving their enemies.**

Jesus' ministry on earth was the perfect example of this spiritual cardio. He spent plenty of time loving his neighbors through good deeds. His ministry on earth included feeding the masses, healing the sick, casting out demons, and even miraculously making wine for a wedding party host who had run out of the good stuff. Jesus worked his spiritual cardio by loving his neighbor, but he also did it by loving his enemies.

A true test of love is how one exercises love in the face of being wronged. In Luke 23, Jesus was led away to an unjust death. Although he never sinned and never wronged anyone on earth, Jesus was condemned to die a criminal's death on the cross. It was a miscarriage of justice, but Jesus did not complain or lash out in anger. He faced God's will for his life with humility. He accepted that he came to die so that sinners could be saved. Jesus even loved the sinners who came to kill him.

As he was being crucified, Jesus prayed to God to forgive his enemies who were executing him. "Jesus said, 'Father, forgive them, for they do not know what they are doing.'" (Luke 23:34) Jesus felt compassion for the Roman soldiers. Perhaps, Jesus knew that after his resurrection, some of the soldiers who were gambling for his clothes would become his followers. Maybe the men who were mocking and taunting him would become faithful servants of the King of Kings and Lord of Lords. In Luke 6, Jesus gives us further insight into God's perspective on the subject of loving your enemies,

> *If you love those who love you, what credit is that to you? Even 'sinners' love those who love them. And if you do good to those who are good to you, what credit is that to you? Even 'sinners' do that. And if you lend to those from whom you expect repayment, what credit is that to you? Even 'sinners' lend to 'sinners' expecting to be repaid in full. But love your enemies, do good to them, and lend to them without expecting to get anything back. Then your reward will be great, and you will be sons of the Most High, because He is kind to the ungrateful and the wicked. Be merciful, just as your Father is merciful.* (Luke 6:32-36)

Spiritual cardio happens when you love those who do *not* love you. It can also happen when you forgive someone who has wronged you. For example, what if your child or spouse was tragically killed in a car accident. Relying on God to help you forgive the person who caused the accident would remove the bitterness and anger that could consume you. Jesus set the example of asking God to forgive the men who were crucifying him while he was dying on the cross. If you ask God to forgive the people in your life who have hurt you or who are presently hurting you, you will be on the road to spiritual transformation. The spiritual cardio of loving your enemy by forgiving them will make you spiritually healthy. Jesus also encourages us to do good works for our enemies. He mentions the act of lending money to them without expecting repayment. Jesus is touching our pocketbook in this illustration and challenging us to be willing to share what is most important to us. This is really hard exercise and challenging spiritual cardio. Loving your enemies is only possible through the work of God's Spirit in your life. As Jesus said, "With man this *is impossible, but with God all things are possible."* (Matthew 19:26)

Summary

You must love your neighbor through acts of kindness and your enemies through good works and by forgiving them. You must help the weak and not despise them, becoming increasingly selfless in the process. You must speak the truth boldly when truth needs to be spoken. The Bible says, *"And we urge you brothers, warn those who are idle, encourage the timid, help the weak, be patient with everyone. Make sure that nobody pays back wrong for wrong, but always try to be kind to each other and to everyone else.* (I Thessalonians 5:14-15) These actions and others will keep your soul healthy and pleasing to God. If you will do this kind of spiritual cardio exercise, you will become truly beautiful like Christ.

Who will you love on purpose today?

Be Intentional

- List some acts of kindness that you can do to show love for neighbors (this would include friends and family).

- Do one of those acts each day until you've completed the list.

- Pick an enemy to pray for today.

- Do an act of kindness for an enemy today based on Jesus' teaching in Luke 6.

- Record how you felt about this in your ESM journal.

Questions for Personal Reflection or Group Study

- How is exercising your soul like exercising your body?

- How did the Good Samaritan and Jesus do spiritual cardio?

- Think of ways that you can do spiritual cardio. Please share.

- Is the person inside of you who is going to live forever a lean, mean, loving machine or a spiritual coach potato?

Day Sixteen
Your Personal Makeover

A Jewel of Transformation: The health and beauty of your soul is tied to exercising you heart through practicing faith, love, forgiveness, and good works.

A Verse to Claim: *"Let us consider how we may spur each other on toward love and good deeds."* (Hebrews 10:24)

A Question to Ponder: How have my faith and good works preserved and helped others around me?

Makeover Tip to Implement: Buy a bag of groceries for your neighbor. Anonymously put it on their porch with a note that God cares for them. Pray for your neighbor. Record how you feel in your ESM journal.

Day 17

Carrying The Burdens of Others

You'll find as I did, that building muscle builds you up in every part of your life.

~Arnold Schwarzenegger

Recent studies show that lifting weights plays an important role in keeping you physically fit. Strength training not only tones your muscles, it also increases your metabolism, reducing body fat. Researchers found that just two sessions of weight training per week can reduce body fat by 3 percent in just 10 weeks, without reducing your calorie intake. Additionally, strength training increases bone mass, which helps prevent osteoporosis. One last benefit is that it exercise releases endorphins that elevate your sense of well-being. The benefits of lifting weights far outweigh the difficulty of this type of exercise. But according to the National Center for

Health Statistics, only 21 percent of women do strength training two or more times a week. We need to start strengthening our muscles by regularly lifting weights.

The same is true of our spiritual muscles. **In order develop a strong inner beauty, we must learn to lift the weight of other's burdens.** While our physical muscles give us the ability to carry heavy objects, our spiritual muscles give us the strength to carry the heavy emotional, mental, and spiritual burdens of those around us. At times, it may feel like the work out is causing micro-tears in our own lives, but these tiny tears heal to make us even stronger, better able to help those in need. Having sculpted, strong spiritual muscles will make you beautiful.

This spiritual weight lifting need not be a "no pain, no gain" proposition. It may be as simple as providing an encouraging word to a friend in a moment of despair, a helpful suggestion when solutions seem distant, or just bringing a fresh perspective to a stale situation. But it can also be as life changing as taking in an orphaned child as your own. We may not be called upon to do the monumental, but we are called upon to do *something,* and usually, that something falls within our gifts or skill set. In addition, your life experiences, no matter your background, may put you in a position of being able to give invaluable help to someone. For example, the book of Titus instructs older women to teach the younger women. Perhaps, you could do this.

Spiritual weight lifting can be seen in shared wisdom, faithful actions, and simple acts of love.

Lifting Weights Through Wise Advice

Sometimes the greatest way to help carry someone's burdens is to help them figure out a way to organize the situation in order to lessen the stress that they are under. Giving wise counsel by helping to organize and plan are fabulous ways to lift the burden of someone who is overwhelmed. The Bible says, *"Carry each other's burdens and in this way you will fulfill the law of Christ."* (Galatians 6:2)

The account of Moses' life contains a story of someone who helped lift an incredible weight off of Moses' shoulders.

After escaping the yoke of slavery in Egypt, the nation of Israel was camped in the desert beyond the reach of the Egyptians. Moses was in charge of approximately one million people. There was no governmental body in place to administer the needs of the people, so the burden of the entire population fell on him. With a million people homeless in the desert, disputes inevitably arose among the people, so they turned to Moses as their judge and arbiter. Needless to say, Moses was overburdened.

Seeing that Moses could not carry such a burden alone, his father-in-law, Jethro, gave some wise counsel:

> *What is this you are doing for the people? Why do you alone sit as judge, while all these people stand around you from morning until evening? What you are doing is not good. You and these people who come to you will only wear yourselves out. The work is too heavy for you; you cannot handle it alone. Listen now to me and I will give you some advice, and may God be with you. You must be the people's representative before God and bring their disputes to him. Teach them his decrees and instructions, and show them the way they are to live and how they are to behave. But select capable men from all the people—men who fear God, trustworthy men who hate dishonest gain—and appoint them as officials over thousands, hundreds, fifties and tens. Have them serve as judges for the people at all times, but have them bring every difficult case to you; the simple cases they can decide themselves. That will make your load lighter, because they will share it with you. If you do this and God so commands, you will be able to stand the strain, and all these people will go home satisfied.* (Exodus 18:14, 17-23)

Jethro was a godly man and by providing Moses with a thoughtful suggestion, he kept Moses from being crushed by the burden he was carrying alone. It is important to note Moses' reaction to Jethro's excellent counsel, *"Moses listened to his father-in-law and did everything he said."* (Exodus 18:24) There will be times when you will be the one in need of help and it will be important for you to be humble enough to accept it.

Lifting Weights Through Faith and Action

Sometimes, the situation requires more than a friend's wise counsel. **There will be times when lifting spiritual weights will mean getting involved and taking action.** In Luke 5, there was a group of friends who did just that. Jesus was teaching some religious leaders in a house when a group of men arrived carrying their paralyzed friend hoping that Christ would heal him. The house was so crowded that they were unable to get through the door. Determined to find a solution, the group carried their friend to the housetop and began to tear a hole in the thatched roof in order to lower their friend down in front of Jesus. It was a bold, loving, and faith-filled act for a friend in need. Jesus was impressed, *"When Jesus saw their faith he said, 'Friend, your sins are forgiven.'"* (Luke 5:20) Then, he healed the man. This man's friends were committed to his well-being. In this case, a simple word of advice would not have provided the needed solution. Instead, these friends rolled up their sleeves, flexed their physical and spiritual muscles, and found a miracle.

A Practical Approach

Sometimes, God enables us to use a simple, practical solution to a problem to bless others. Look, for example, at this scenario.

> *Jennifer loved to be involved. When two of her three children began elementary school, she eagerly volunteered at their school. As a reading volunteer, room mother, and cafeteria monitor, she was pleased to be part of her children's educational experience.*
>
> *As a Christian, Jennifer also felt it was important to be active in her church. On Sundays, she taught first grade Sunday school and helped with the children's choir. During the week, she prepared meals, cleaned the house, changed diapers, bandaged boo boo's, and chauffeured her kids to various activities. Jennifer was blessed, but tired.*
>
> *One morning while talking to a girlfriend on the phone, Jennifer realized that she was not the only one experiencing the feeling of being overwhelmed. She and her friend decided to start a meal-sharing group. Each lady would cook one meal a week and make*

> *enough of it for the seven families in the meal-sharing bunch. Then, the ladies would exchange meals with each other and only have to cook one day a week. Having dinner provided by other people most of the week gave Jennifer some much needed rest.*

Can you think of someone who might need help with a hectic life? Can you help carry their burden by creatively sharing responsibilities? This is an important concept to practice within your family. Developing strong spiritual muscles may mean learning to share responsibilities with each other.

In order to be spiritually fit, we must exercise our spiritual muscles by sharing responsibilities with someone who is overburdened, giving godly advice, having coffee with a friend to talk about life, or meeting the physical needs of someone who is hurting. Take the time to help carry the burdens of those around you. When you do this, you will be developing beauty that lasts!

Be Intentional

- Take time to call a person who may need your advice.
- Have coffee with an old friend to catch up on life.
- If you live far away from someone with whom you

need to reconnect, Skype with him or her over the Internet to let that person know you care about his or her life.

- Visit someone in the hospital this week.

- Take a friend to a Bible study or church and share the good news of Christ with them this week.

Questions for Personal Reflection or Group Study

- How can you become a spiritual weight lifter?

- Share some ways that you can help carry the burden of some of the people in your life.

- How can you carry someone to the feet of Jesus, spiritually, like the friends of the paralytic man did?

- Think about how to spend more time helping others with their needs rather than complaining about your own burdens. How will this make your inner person more beautiful?

Day Seventeen
Your Personal Makeover

A Jewel of Transformation: The act of helping other people in need will build your spiritual muscles and make you eternally beautiful.

A Verse to Claim: *"Carry each other's burdens and in this way you will fulfill the law of Christ."* (Galatians 6:2)

A Question to Ponder: How can I show mercy to someone today?

Makeover Tip to Implement: Take a meal to someone in need.

Day 18
It's A Marathon

Since we are surrounded by such a great cloud of witnesses, let us throw off everything that hinders and the sin that so easily entangles, and let us run with perseverance the race marked out for us.

~Hebrews 12:1

Powered by Hope

    I recently had the privilege of attending the Ironman competition in Kona, Hawaii. I say it was a privilege because it was an opportunity to watch the incredible determination, focus, and will that some are able to draw upon to accomplish amazing feats. In case you have never heard of it, the best way to describe the Ironman is that it is an epic, full day and night mega-race designed to test the limits of human athleticism. It is a triathlon where the competitors swim 2.4 miles in the open ocean, ride 112 miles by bike, and run 26.2 miles all without stopping. To watch these athletes persist through pain and hardship is to see endurance personified.

It would have been special enough to go to the beautiful island of Hawaii to watch complete strangers do this race, but I was able to go and support a very close friend of mine who was competing in this triathlon while battling stage 4-colon cancer. My friend's name is Teri Griege, and Teri is a woman of faith, **who is powered by hope**.

As a life-long athlete, Teri was used to competition and had spent many hours training, making her very fit and healthy. So it was a shock when she was diagnosed with stage 4-colon cancer that had metastasized to her liver giving her only a six percent chance of surviving for 5 years. It would have been easy for her to give up in the face of this news, but never one to shy away from a challenge, after her surgery and initial chemo treatments, Teri slapped on a fanny pack containing a pump that infused her with chemotherapy drugs and began fifty-mile bike rides to train for the Ironman competition. To say she is inspiring is to not do her justice. With guts and determination, Teri swam in the open waters of the ocean, biked through the island's lava fields, and ran through the streets of Kona, completing the Ironman with family and friends watching in the stands. It was a glorious sight to watch her cross the finish line after overcoming so many physical and emotional hardships. It was a testimony to endurance, a testimony to hope, and a testimony that with God all things are possible.

Your Christian life is also a race. The Bible indicates that your race, like the Ironman Competition, is not some quick sprint, but an all-consuming test of endurance in which you will face unforeseen difficulties and overcome countless hardships. Your spiritual life is the ultimate marathon. But even in the face of difficulties, you are assured victory through Jesus Christ. Scripture gives us the keys to achieving the promised victory in the book of Hebrews.

Embrace the Race

In Hebrews 12, believers are admonished to embrace the race!

> *Therefore, since we are surrounded by such a great cloud of witnesses, let us throw off everything that hinders and the sin that so easily entangles. And let us run with perseverance the race marked out for us, fixing our eyes on Jesus, the pioneer and perfecter of faith. For the joy set before him he endured the cross, scorning its shame, and sat down at the right hand of the throne of God. Consider him who endured such opposition from sinners, so that you will not grow weary and lose heart.* (Hebrews 12:1-3)

First, we must **recognize** that spiritually, we have **a cloud of witnesses** who have passed from this world to the next, who are able to watch us as we run our spiritual marathon in this life. Just as I felt privileged to watch my friend, Teri, run her race, believers who have completed their faith journey are now in the presence of Christ and are privileged observers of you and me as we run the race marked out for us. Notice that each of us has a unique race that is marked out for us by God. The race you're called to run may look very different from the race your neighbor is called to run. You are being watched by your Christian brothers and sisters who have run before you, and this should motivate you to run *your* race well. As these past heroes of the faith are watching your race, what are they seeing?

Second, the passage tells us to **throw off everything that hinders us.** In the ancient world prior to the fourth century AD, athletes competed in some athletic events in the nude. They would throw off all of their clothing in order to be free from anything that might slow them down. This is what the author of Hebrews is talking about. What hinders your ability to run your race of faith each day? Perhaps you are weighed down by anxiety and worry. These burdens are like heavy clothing that prevents free movement. Throw off these tendencies. Maybe bitterness is slowing you down. Learn to forgive others and let go of your anger. Run your race free from these burdens.

Third, we are to **get rid of the sin that can entangle us.** Sin is like a net that catches you up and prevents you from making progress in the race. You need to let go of sin, break free from old habits, so you can run like the wind. What sin might be entangling you today?

Fourth, success in this spiritual race will come if we **fix our eyes upon Jesus** as we run. Athletes learn early on to fix their eyes on the prize in order to stay motivated. It helps in a marathon to look to the next goal that you must reach. Perhaps a mile marker or a landmark in the distance can keep the athlete moving forward. The author of Hebrews states that Jesus is our mile marker. *"Let us fix our eyes on Jesus, the author and perfecter of our faith, who for the joy set before him endured the cross, scorning its shame, and sat down at the right hand of the throne of God."* (Hebrews 12:2-4) We are to fix our eyes upon Him. Jesus is our example of how to win the race.

Fifth, we must learn to **have a proper focus**. What did Jesus focus on in order to endure the cross? We are told that he concentrated on the joy of his future glorification and reunion with God. This focus helped him to face the scorn and shame of the cross before sitting down on his throne in heaven. Remember that you, too, are promised a reunion with God in a glorified body. You'll spend eternity with the Lord in a new heaven and earth where there will be no more tears and no more sorrow (Revelation 21). The Bible encourages you to focus on this truth as you run your race.

True faith leads a person to run their spiritual race with endurance, even in the face of hardships. The Bible says, *"Consider it pure joy, my brothers, whenever you face trials of many kinds, because you know that the testing of your faith develops perseverance. Perseverance must finish its work so that you may be mature and complete, not lacking anything."* (James 1:2-4) God loves you so much that He even uses the hard things in your life to shape your character. It is never easy to run a marathon, to believe in things that you cannot see, or to endure discipline as a child of God, but follow Christ's example and run your spiritual marathon with faith. This is how you will develop beauty that lasts forever.

Be Intentional

- In your ESM journal, list past hardships that you have experienced in your life.

- Now, list present hardships that you are enduring.

- Transfer these lists to index cards and lay them out like your life has been a marathon race.

- How has God disciplined you through these hardships? Record your responses in your journal.

- How has God preserved you through these hardships and even brought you to victory over the difficulties? Record this, too.

Questions for Personal Reflection or Group Study

- What inspired you about Teri's story?

- How is your Christian life like a spiritual marathon?

- What is hindering your race and needs to be thrown off?

- How are you remembering to use Jesus as a spiritual mile marker and what goal will you reach at the finish line?

- Consider how the hardships in your life are like spiritual training. According to the Bible, what is this training producing in you?

Day Eighteen
Your Personal Makeover

A Jewel of Transformation: Life is a marathon of faith with victory in Christ guaranteed for those who love God. As you run your spiritual race, faith in God, obedience to His Word, and trust in His goodness and love will help you to endure life's hardships and God's disciplines.

A Verse to Claim: *"Thanks be to God who gives us the victory through our Lord Jesus Christ."* (I Corinthians 15:57-58)

A Question to Ponder: What should I throw off that hinders me in my race of faith?

Makeover Tip to Implement: Take a long walk or run. Use the time to talk to God about hardships you have endured. Remember to thank Him for the hardships!

Dressed for Success

Adornment is never anything except a reflection of the heart.

~Coco Chanel

Day 19
The Believer's Closet

Decorate yourself from the inside out.

~Terri Gullemets

Some things just naturally go together like peanut butter and jelly, pen and paper, and women and clothing. When my daughter was little, her favorite dolls were called Polly Pockets. Perfect for my little fashionista, each small Polly doll came in a clear handbag containing several outfits and matching accessories. The bags were themed, so one doll might have beach outfits and accessories like swim suits and flip-flops, while another Polly would be in a party themed bag with a variety of dresses, little matching purses, and itty-bitty high heels. My daughter would pretend that the beach Polly was a sassy, athletic girl with a spunky personality, while the party girl was more sophisticated and creative. She had what seemed like hundreds of tiny outfits to put on her floor-full-of Polly dolls and each outfit presented an opportunity to assign a new personality to her little friends.

What Are You Wearing?

Just as my daughter chose how to dress her dolls each day to reflect their pretend personalities, when you and I go into our closets to pick an outfit to wear we are intentionally choosing how we want to present ourselves to the world. Your clothing might express that you are a strong professional woman, a busy soccer mom, a femme fatal, or a dedicated athlete. The same is true of the character qualities that you choose to clothe your personality in each day. As you make the intentional choices to clothe yourself with the qualities of Christ, you tell the world who you are spiritually.

The Bible says, *"Your beauty should not come from outward adornment, such as braided hair and the wearing of gold jewelry and fine clothes. Instead, it should be that of your inner self, the unfading beauty of a gentle and quiet spirit, which is of great worth in God's sight."* (I Peter 3:3-4) If you are being transformed into the image of Christ, the beauty of his character will be the lovely outfit your personality is clothed in each day.

A Robe Of Righteousness

Clothing is often mentioned in the Bible as a symbol for being either acceptable or unacceptable to God. Before being saved, your righteous acts and good deeds are described in Isaiah 64:6 as being nothing more than filthy rags. But having come to a saving relationship with Jesus Christ, your faith positions you before God in a robe of righteousness. *"I am overwhelmed with joy in the Lord my God! For he has dressed me with the clothing of salvation and draped me in a robe of righteousness. I am like a bridegroom in his wedding suit or a bride with her jewels."* (Isaiah 61:10) God cares about how you look in your inner person. With Christ's help, you now wear clean white linen and are a jeweled bride acceptable to Christ. What a beautiful picture!

Each day, you should remind yourself that you are a jeweled bride in white linen, dressed to shine forth to the world. You have reason to hold your head high. You are well loved. This is your day.

A Full Closet

With this fabulous beginning, you can now decide what other beautiful traits to put on in order to properly accessorize your look. The Bible is full of teachings on how to live in a way that pleases God and develops your image to match the beauty of Christ's. Let's look at some of the Scriptures that encourage us to dress well each day.

Job 29:14-17 – Righteousness and Justice

"I put on righteousness as my clothing; justice was my robe and my turban. I was eyes to the blind and feet to the lame. I was a father to the needy; I took up the case of the stranger. I broke the fangs of the wicked and snatched the victims from their teeth." (Job 29:14-17)

When Job chose to wear righteousness and justice each day, it resulted in him making a big difference in his community. Clothed in these qualities, Job met the concerns of the needy, defended the downtrodden, and rescued widows and orphans from the clutches of evil. This is intentional living. Cloaking himself in the Christ-like qualities of righteousness and justice made Job a beautiful person. The good works in his life were evidence of his beauty. As an Extreme Spiritual Makeover candidate, you should choose to put on righteousness and justice each day.

Proverbs 31:25 – Strength and Dignity

"She is clothed with strength and dignity; she can laugh at the days to come. She speaks with wisdom, and faithful instruction is on her tongue." (Proverbs 31:25-26)

Here, we have the wife of noble character. Where did she acquire her strength and dignity? How is it that she has the confidence to laugh about the future? Her strength and dignity are found in the believer's closet of strong faith in God. It is through faith that we face our daily trials with grace.

But, how many of us are living stressed out lives worrying about what is coming tomorrow or the next month? There is a great quote that says, *"Today is the tomorrow you worried about yesterday."* Consider whether you have truly clothed yourself in the strength and dignity that comes from faith in God. When your hope truly rests in Jesus Christ and the promise of eternal life with Him, you will have the confidence to laugh at the days to come because you know how God's story ends. It is a confidence based in the fact that Jesus is victorious over his enemies and even over death itself. If God is for us, who can be against us? Truly, what is there to worry about?

Being clothed with strength and dignity will cause *you* to develop the wisdom of Christ in you. That is really dressing for success.

Luke 24:49 – Power

"I am going to send you what my Father has promised; but stay in the city until you have been clothed with power from on high." (Luke 24:49)

Perhaps you feel that your life is out of control. You may feel like you spend your time being knocked around by the circumstances of your life. If so, the words that Jesus said to his disciples should bring you great comfort.

It was God's intention all along to provide you with the power to make changes in your life and to have His supernatural ability to cope with trials and circumstances. This power is available through the Holy Spirit. There is an expectation that once you receive this power, you will use it to conform to the image of Christ. Remember when Jesus told the woman caught in adultery to go and sin no more? He expected her to conform to God's image. This means watching how Christ handled daily interactions and trials. This means praying to God to inspire you to utilize the power He has given you.

Being clothed with power from on high is a great way to start your day. Responding to the Holy Spirit is key to wearing power from on high.

Colossians 3:12 – Compassion, Kindness, Humility, Gentleness, and Patience

"Therefore, as God's chosen people, holy and dearly loved, clothe yourselves with compassion, kindness, humility, gentleness and patience." (Colossians 3:12)

This is a key verse for understanding the believer's closet. Becoming beautiful like Christ is a choice you make every day. It is literally like picking the outfit you will wear. Each day, because you are chosen by God to be His child, He expects you to pick these attitudes to wear. You are holy by position. Christ's death and resurrection has put you in the position of being righteous before God. **Now, it is time to start becoming holy in your behavior, so that your actions will match your position of righteousness.**

As you choose to put on compassion for other people, you will begin to look like Jesus. Are you kind to others? What about being humble and not retaliating against those who offend you? Remember how Jesus prayed for the men who were crucifying him? Jesus did not lash out at them, but instead, clothed himself with humility.

Are you gentle with people who are sinful and frail, or do you judge others harshly? Putting on gentleness is something that will cause you to act like Christ. Who do you know that needs your gentleness today?

"Patience is a virtue." Have you heard this saying? It's true, but patience is hard to master in our hectic, fast-paced world. Sitting in traffic can lead a person to lose patience. Having a jam-packed schedule and a child who is not getting dressed in time for school can cause one to lose patience. Watching someone ruin their life through addiction can cause one to lose patience. How can you clothe yourself in patience today? Who will benefit from you dressing this way?

The believer's closet is full of beautiful things to wear. You cannot go wrong putting on compassion, kindness, humility, gentleness, or patience on any given day. Give it a try!

I Peter 5:5 – Humility

"All of you, clothe yourselves with humility toward one another, because, 'God opposes the proud but gives grace to the humble.'"(I Peter 5:5)

The Apostle Paul is quoting Proverbs 3:34. When we clothe ourselves with humility, we are admitting that we don't know it all. We recognize that we are weak and flawed. Is this something that you realize about yourself? How does realizing that you are weak cause you to rely on God to make you strong in your faith? How does realizing that you are weak make you more gracious towards others who are also weak?

Do you see how clothing yourself with humility opens you up to God's intervention in your life? Recognizing that God has been patient and grace-filled towards you in your weakness and sin helps you to be gracious to others who are weak and sinful. Because God has forgiven us, we should be humble enough to afford others that same grace. We did not deserve God's grace, so we should be humble enough to extend grace to others, even if we think they don't deserve it. Doing so fulfills Jesus' admonition in the Lord's Prayer to forgive others as we have been forgiven.

Acknowledging that God is in control of this universe and you are not enables you to clothe yourself in humility. It helps you to forgive others as you have been forgiven. It is gives you the ability to be gracious to other people. Humility is the opposite of pride. Pride will lead you to attack an enemy. Humility will lead you to pray for an enemy.

Jesus wore a cloak of humility every second of his life on earth. Why don't you put on humility today?

Reorganizing Your Closet

Closet organization is a growth industry in this country. People seem to have more clothes than closet space. The believer's closet is also packed with great things to wear.

Are you ever an outfit repeater? We are quick to frown on someone who shows up at a party wearing an outfit they've worn before, but we tend to be less critical of ourselves when we are repeatedly wearing the same old sinful habits each day. It is those sinful attitudes and actions that must be thrown out. Don't wear them anymore. Don't be a sinful attitude outfit repeater!

God calls you to put on Jesus Christ daily. Your life should reflect the righteousness, justice, mercy, kindness, humility, gentleness, and patience that only Christ can provide. Wearing these "clothes" each day will make you beautiful. This is the kind of beauty that will last!

Be Intentional

- Find a charity that meets a need that you feel is important. Begin to volunteer with that charity.

- Stand up for someone who is being bullied or abused. Protect the downtrodden.

- Find a way to help the unborn babies in your community. Make sure that they are having an opportunity to live. Remember, they are defenseless.

- Take off one bad/sinful attitude each day and purpose to not wear it again. Put on one godly attitude instead.

- Respond with gentle words to someone who attacks you.

- Do not judge someone who is weak in his or her character. Pray for them, instead. Why not find a way to help them overcome his or her weakness in some practical way?

Questions for Personal Reflection or Group Study

- Think of an example of how your clothes have represented something about your personality. Share what that outfit was and what it reflected.

- Pick clothes from the believer's closet that you want to put on each day. Share which ones you picked and why you picked them.

- Explain how these can make you attractive to other people and to God?

- How can you begin to stop being a sinful attitude outfit repeater? What bad attitude will you purpose to stop wearing each day?

Day Nineteen
Your Personal Makeover

A Jewel of Transformation: You must clothe yourself with the qualities of Christ each day in order to really dress for success.

A Verse to Claim: *"Clothe yourself with the Lord Jesus Christ."* (Romans 13:14)

A Question to Ponder: How can I wear the qualities of Christ each day?

Makeover Tip to Implement: Write down one of your favorite qualities about Jesus' personality. Purpose to put on that quality today. Write about it in your journal.

Day 20
An Attitude of Gratitude

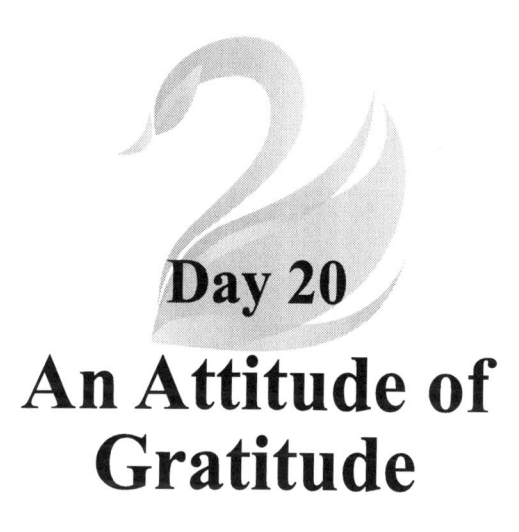

Enter His gates with thanksgiving and his courts with praise; give thanks to Him and praise His name.

~Psalm 100:4

"*You deserve a break today. So get up and get away to McDonalds.*" Advertising works. If you spend any time listening to the radio or television, you will more than likely spend money you would not have and make decisions that you might otherwise never have considered because advertisers are bombarding you with clever jingles designed to entice you to want more things. Much of the advertising is designed to appeal to the base human tendencies that are as old as humanity itself.

One of those base tendencies is the tendency for humans to feel entitled. Somehow, deep within ourselves we feel that we deserve a good life with no suffering. We are disappointed when we are not healthy, loved, wealthy, and free from trials and suffering. This attitude of entitlement leads to disillusionment because life in this fallen world is not fair. Another tendency is to never be satisfied with what we have. We want to want to "keep up with the Joneses." This attitude of entitlement reflects a wrong perspective.

If we live our lives thinking that someone owes us something and that a human institution, such as government, will be able to solve the problems of inequality in our societies, we will find that rather than creating a Utopian paradise of beauty and order, we will instead create chaos and envy because the attitude of entitlement is insatiable. God's perspective is different. **In order for the Extreme Spiritual Makeover candidate to become spiritually beautiful and reflect God's image in her life, she must adopt a personal attitude of gratitude.**

Wearing a Garment of Gratitude

Thankfulness is an important steppingstone on the path to a proper perspective on life. Being grateful reflects a gracious heart that appreciates what has been done for you. Gratitude is something that you should put on each day, intentionally. Being grateful will make you more eternally beautiful and happy.

The Bible gives us an example of putting on an attitude of gratitude in the seventeenth chapter of Luke. Jesus was on his way to Jerusalem. *"As he was going into a village, ten men who had leprosy met him. They stood at a distance and called out in a loud voice, 'Jesus, Master, have pity on us.'"* (Luke 17:12) Leprosy is a chronic infectious disease that when left untreated causes nerve damage, numbness, festering wounds on the hands and feet, and deformities of the face and limbs. If you had this disease in the ancient Jewish world, you were considered unclean and a cast out from society, unable to participate in worship or community.

These ten leprous men called out for Jesus to have pity on them because word had gotten around that Jesus could heal the sick. Responding to their pleas, Jesus simply told them to go show themselves to the priests, which was the protocol for proving that they were healthy and able to rejoin the community. As the men left to go to the priests, demonstrating their faith that Jesus could heal them, they were, indeed, cleansed.

After being cleansed, one of the ten men returned to thank Jesus. *"One of them when he saw that he was healed, came back, praising God in a loud voice. He threw himself at Jesus' feet and thanked him – and he was a Samaritan."* (Luke 17: 15-16) This man was dramatic in his gratitude. Interestingly, the passage points out that this man is a Samaritan. You will recall that the Jews despised the Samaritans, yet Jesus seemed to purposefully interact with them. His message was that he had come to save those who seek him, whether Jew, Samaritan, or Gentile.

Struck by the fact that only one man returned to thank him, Jesus asks, *"Were not all ten cleansed? Where are the other nine? Was no one found to return and give praise to God except this foreigner?"* (Luke 17:17-18) Notice that Jesus expected to be thanked for healing the men. It is God's expectation that we have gratitude for all that He has done for us. Jesus commended the man for returning to thank him, and told the man that his faith has made him well.

It was the Samaritan, not the Jewish men, who stepped onto the path of thankfulness and wore a garment of gratitude. The Samaritan will live forever because of his faith in Christ. His thankfulness was evidence of his faith.

Gratitude to God is evidence of faith in God. This is beauty that will last forever.

Gratitude is a Testimony

An attitude of gratitude is beautiful because it is a testimony of what someone else has done for you, rather than what *you* have done for yourself. We see this principle illustrated in the nineteenth chapter of Luke when Jesus is approaching the town of Jericho. As usual, a crowd was following Christ. There was a blind man begging on the side of the road that heard the commotion and upon learning that Jesus of Nazareth was passing by, cried out, *"Jesus, Son of David, have mercy on me!"* (Luke 18:39) Let's note two things at this point. First, the blind man refers to Jesus as the "Son of

David." This reference to Jesus' lineage indicates that the blind man believes that Jesus is the promised Savior. Second, notice that the beggar does not have an attitude of entitlement. He does not demand that Jesus heal him because he deserves it in some way. Instead, he humbly pleads for God's mercy.

Others in the crowd rebuked the beggar and tried to get him to shut up and stop bothering Jesus. It didn't work. The blind man shouted all the more. Jesus heard him and ordered that the man be brought to him. When the man humbly requested to be healed, *"Jesus said to him, 'Receive your sight; your faith has healed you.'"* (Luke 18:42) The man's response was one of gratitude. He immediately began to follow Jesus, praising God all along. *"When all the people saw it, they also praised God."* (Luke 18:43) His grateful attitude was infectious, causing others in the crowd to also begin praising God. This humble beggar's thankfulness was a testimony and his attitude of gratitude drew others to God. This is a beauty that will last forever.

Gratitude Changes Perspective

A man who is eating or lying with his wife or preparing to go to sleep in humility, thankfulness and temperance, is, by Christian standards, in an infinitely higher state than one who is listening to Bach or reading Plato in a state of pride.

~C. S. Lewis

Thankfulness and gratitude are game changers for the Christian. **How we think determines how we act.** Gratitude will change your life. Thinking about how grateful you are for what you have, rather than being resentful for what you do not have, is the difference between being beautiful in your soul and being ugly in your soul. Rather than feeling entitled and cheated, you can feel empowered and blessed. Sharing your gratitude about God with others will empower them to realize their own blessings. Here is a thought to consider, "It is not the happy person who is thankful, but the thankful person who is happy." Why not put on an attitude of gratitude each day? This starts a process that affects change.

Be Intentional

Take time to create an Attitude of Gratitude garment list. These are items that can adorn your daily wardrobe. Divide the list into the following categories:

- Thankful for God.

- Thankful for God's Story found in His Word.

- Thankful for my life, which is part of God's grand Story.

- Thankful for truth.

- Thankful for this world, even though there are troubles here.

- Thankful for family and friends.

- Thankful for trials and suffering.

- Thankful for the promised future in eternity.

Questions for Personal Reflection or Group Study

- Explain what feeling entitled means.

- How is thankfulness part of humility?

- How is gratitude a testimony to God?

- Describe how gratitude in your life might change things for the better.

- What are you thankful for?

Day Twenty
Your Personal Makeover

A Jewel of Transformation: Wearing an attitude of gratitude will make you eternally beautiful because you will feel empowered and blessed.

A Verse to Claim: *"But in all things give thanks."* (I Thessalonians 5:8)

A Question to Ponder: How can I be a more grateful person?

Makeover Tip to Implement: Write a note of thanks to someone who has made a difference in your life. Mail the note today. Write that person's name and this date in your ESM journal.

Day 21
Dressed For Battle

Finally, be strong in the Lord and in his mighty power.

Put on the full armor of God so that you can

Take your stand against the devil's schemes.

~Ephesians 6:10-11

Part of your Extreme Spiritual Makeover is realizing that you are in a battle every day. You face unseen obstacles and enemies that never sleep. Every day is filled with struggles and strife. Worse yet, you are battling against actual forces of evil. This battle rages on every minute of every hour of every day while you are alive on planet Earth.

The Bible describes the nature of this epic battle in Ephesians chapter 6, *"For our struggle is not against flesh and blood, but against the rulers, against the authorities, against the powers of this dark world and against the spiritual forces of evil in the heavenly realms."* (Ephesians 6:12) This passage clarifies that Satan and his fallen angels are often behind many of the conflicts, both mental and emotional, that we have within ourselves and with other people. In other words, there is often more than meets the eye behind the various difficulties that we face in our lives. While there are physical manifestations of this struggle, it is important to keep in mind that this is primarily a spiritual war.

So how does this battle manifest itself in our lives? There are a variety of ways including:

- All manner of temptations
- Interpersonal conflicts with others
- Lies in our heads about our self-worth and ability to be loved by God and others
- Negative coping mechanisms for our pain including addictions, self-harm, and abusive behaviors
- Bitterness and difficulty forgiving others
- All forms of envy, strife and anger
- Immoral sexual behavior

God has not left us to fend for ourselves against Satan's assault. He does not expect us to engage in this battle without protection. You need to suit up to defend yourself. How do you do that? **Very simply, the greatest means you have of battling these forces is the truth found in Scripture.**

God's Gear

Any time you play a sport, you need to wear the right equipment. Growing up, my son played ice hockey. He was the goalie and, as you might imagine, he never stepped onto the ice without first putting on his helmet, pads, gloves, mouthpiece, and skates. He also made sure to have his goalie stick with him. This is the only way that he could stand against the onslaught of whizzing hockey pucks he would face during the game. Just as my son needed to be suited up properly for his game, you need to be dressed properly for your daily battle.

Wearing the right battle gear will prepare you to come up against the forces of evil that mess with your head every day. The Apostle Paul wrote a letter to the church in Ephesus that outlines what you should put on each day in order to be prepared to fight. This gear is designed to help you take a stand against the Devil's strategies. You saw how Satan tempted Christ in the desert. Please realize that if Satan tried to tempt Jesus, the very Son of God, he will surely try to tempt you.

Paul instructs believers to put on spiritual armor each day so that first and foremost, believers can stand their ground. Sometimes, when you are in a difficult fight, the best result is to have withstood the assault and not lost any ground. That is what the Apostle Paul is saying. *"Therefore put on the full armor of God, so that when the day of evil comes, you may be able to stand your ground, and after you have done everything, to stand."* (Ephesians 6:13) Paul then lists the equipment God has issued to protect us in battle.

> *Stand firm then, with the belt of truth buckled around your waist, with the breastplate of righteousness in place, and with your feet fitted with the readiness that comes from the gospel of peace. In addition to all this, take up the shield of faith, with which you can extinguish all the flaming arrows of the evil one. Take the helmet of salvation and the sword of the Spirit, which is the word of God.* (Ephesians 6:13-17)

First, you must put on the **belt of Truth**. Here is your equipment to combat lies. With the belt of Truth on your waist, you can combat the lies that Satan tries to put into your head each day. This would include lies about God and lies about you. Maybe he's telling you that you are not good enough, that you cannot be forgiven for what you have done in the past, or that you are worthless. These are the sorts of lies that Satan, "the Accuser," promotes. One of his purposes is to make you doubt yourself and doubt God. If you are wearing the belt of Truth, you will be able to tell the difference between God's truth and Satan's lies so that you can fend off these lies, and rest in the truth of God's Word.

Second, over your heart, you are to wear the **breastplate of righteousness**. Christ died so that you would be in a position of righteousness before God. With your sins forgiven and removed in God's mind, God sees you as righteous. Protect your heart with this concept. Don't let Satan tell you that you are unforgivable. It's a lie.

Third, your shoes for this battle are the **boots of the gospel of peace**. These boots plant you on the battlefield with the good news of peace. The gospel, or good news, is that you are now at peace with God. Nothing can separate you from eternity with Him. Do not believe the lies that you can lose your salvation. Stand firm in your boots of the gospel of peace.

Fourth, do not forget to take up the **shield of faith**. Hoping in the truth will extinguish the flaming arrows of doubt that Satan loves to shoot. He would like for you to doubt God's love, mercy, patience, and the promise of eternity. Don't buy the lie. Keep up your shield of faith and have confidence in the goodness of God.

Fifth, over your precious head, you must wear the **helmet of salvation**. Protecting your mind with the truth that you have been saved from death by Christ is crucial. Your salvation is real and you must protect your mind with this truth.

Sixth, your offensive weapon is the **sword of the Word of God**. Scripture can be thought of as the essence of God explained on paper. Nothing will wound your enemy, the Devil, like the truth about God. Jesus used this sword in the desert when he was tempted. He quoted Scripture to Satan and it caused Satan to flee. You must use this sword each day to chase evil from your life.

Finally, once you are dressed for battle, you must pray. Prayer changes things. As you go into the battle of life each day, consult with God and ask for His help.

Each day before you face temptations and come against unseen forces of evil, suit up properly in your battle gear, rely on God's truth, and never retreat. Fight the good fight, and become a beautiful person in the process.

Be Intentional

- Purpose to fight the temptation to participate in negative talk inside your head about yourself.

- Decide to forgive yourself for past sins, as God has.

- March into battle today by sharing the gospel of peace with someone who needs to hear some good news.

- Believe that God loves you. Act like you are loved.

- Renew your mind and put on the belt of truth by thinking about what your salvation means to you.

- Memorize a verse about God's love and say it to yourself.
- Pray on purpose today.

Questions for Personal Reflection or Group Study

- Explain what the spiritual battle is that you face each day.
- How does this battle manifest itself in your thoughts and attitudes?
- Which piece of God's armor do you value the most and why?
- How does salvation act as a helmet to your mind and thinking?
- Explain how the Word of God act like a sword that cuts sin out of your life.
- How is wearing this battle gear going to make you more beautiful?

Day Twenty-One
Your Personal Makeover

A Jewel of Transformation: You can fight temptation and doubt by wearing the full armor of God.

A Verse to Claim: *"Finally, be strong in the Lord and in his mighty power."* (Ephesians 6:10)

A Question to Ponder: How can I fight temptation in my life each day?

Makeover Tip to Implement: Write out some lies that you tell yourself on a piece of paper. Go to the Bible and pick verses that reflect the truth. Put on a belt and state the Biblical truths out loud as you buckle the belt. Write the truths on a different piece of paper. Now, tear up the paper with the lies and throw them away.

Budgeting For Beauty

Beauty saves. Beauty heals.

Beauty motivates. Beauty unites.

Beauty returns us to our origins,

and here lies the ultimate act of saving,

of healing, of overcoming...

~Matthew Fox

Day 22

The Cost of Obedience

Only he who believes is obedient and only he who is obedient believes.

~Dietrich Bonhoeffer

According to the nonprofit YWCA, women and girls in the United States are spending approximately $8 billion dollars a year in pursuit of beauty. The obsessive desire to look like the air-brushed models in the magazines is increasing the sales of cosmetic products and popularizing cosmetic surgery procedures, even for teens. The report, *Beauty At Any Cost*, estimated that an average of $100 a month was spent on beauty products for every woman and girl in America. In my opinion, $100 per month would be on the low side considering the cost of getting your hair and nails done, in addition to paying for products like shampoos, make up, and lotions. Regardless, the point is that we are willing to pay the price for physical beauty without batting an eye.

As an Extreme Spiritual Makeover candidate, just as you budget your money to various things in order to make yourself physically beautiful, you should budget time, effort, and finances in order to develop your spiritual beauty. For example, you may plan to spend $100 each month to have your hair done at the salon, but you have never budgeted a quiet time to read the Bible and pray to God daily. It will cost you time away from other activities to budget in the obedience of prayer and time alone with God. Perhaps you spend $150 a month at Starbucks, obeying Christ may mean allotting some of that money to a ministry, such as Compassion International, to help a child in need.

The cost of obedience to Christ could be much more significant, though. You may be called upon to forgo a business opportunity at work because it would compromise your integrity. Maybe the cost of obedience will mean refusing to participate in cruel gossip, which may strain personal friendships and lead to you losing a friendship in the end. But what if the cost of obeying Christ was even greater?

Laying Down a Life

Would you be willing to obey God even if it cost you your life? A martyr is someone who dies for a cause. The first recorded Christian martyr was a man named Stephen. Stephen's obedience to Christ cost him his life because his public teachings about Jesus got him on the enemies' list of certain powerful Jews. Instead of obeying the Jewish authorities, who wanted testimony about Jesus being the promised Messiah quashed, Stephen obeyed Christ's admonition, *"Go into all the world and preach the good news to all creation."* (Mark 16:15)

Infuriated by his pointed sermons, the crowd dragged Stephen to the Jewish religious council to be judged for blasphemy. Stephen accused the religious leaders of being stiff-necked people with uncircumcised hearts and ears. This description questioned the authenticity of their faith in God. Enraged, they stoned him to death. With his face looking like that of an angel's, Stephen's last words indicated that he saw the heavens open and Jesus standing at the right hand of God. He asked Jesus to forgive his enemies and then, he died. Stephen's obedience to God's call to preach the gospel of Christ cost him his life.

You may think that people being willing to die for Christ is something that only happened in the past, but there is a pastor in modern day Iran who is presently facing the death penalty because of his faith. Youcef Nadarkhani was jailed in 2009 in Lakan Province, Iran because he approached his son's school district to protest mandatory Islamic classes on the Koran that his son was forced to take. As a Christian, this father did not want the Islamic religion to be part of his child's mandatory curriculum. For standing up for his beliefs, Pastor Nadarkhani was jailed for apostasy. This obedient servant of Christ might die for following his convictions. When asked to renounce Christ in order to obtain a release from jail, this brave man refused. His obedience to God has cost Youcef Nadarkhani his freedom and may end up costing him his life.

But Christians do not always face death for their obedience. More often than not, they just count the cost of looking like a fool to the unbelieving world.

Looking Like A Fool

Sometimes, obedience to God will cause you to look like a fool to others. One of the costs of obeying Jesus' teachings is that we will often look out of step with our contemporaries. The Bible says, *"For the message of the cross is foolishness to those who are perishing, but to us who are being saved it is the power of God."* (1 Corinthians 1:18) People may not like it if you are acting differently than them by, for example, abstaining from alcohol, refraining from sex outside of marriage, or simply being different because you stand up for biblical principles that the world finds dated and irrelevant. Perhaps you don't let your children watch certain television shows or movies because those shows do not promote good morals or respect for parents. In your desire to avoid evil as Christ commanded, you may feel ostracized among your peers. Looking different is sometimes a cost of obedience to Christ.

There is a group of teenagers in St. Louis, Missouri who count the cost of obedience each time they do a presentation in a high school about the consequences of teens making bad decisions. This group is called *BreakDown STL* and was started by Jenna Imergoot. Using dance, drama, and video testimonies, this group grapples with difficult cultural topics including sex, bullying, self-harm, abusive relationships, alcohol abuse, and drug use. While many teens are trying to fit in with their peers by engaging in these behaviors, the members of *BreakDown STL* are standing apart from their culture to speak truth. Instead of giving into peer pressure and giving up on being obedient to Scripture, this inspiring group is helping to shape their culture, one life at a time. They are prompted by their faith to call their generation to healthy living. They are willing to look like fools to their peers in order to stand up for what is right. This is the cost of obedience.

Looking like a fool is what happened to Noah when God commanded him to build the Ark so many millennia ago. In the face of an evil generation, Noah and his family spent one hundred years building an enormous multi-decked barge at God's command. The Bible says, *"Noah did everything just as God commanded him."* (Genesis 6:22) Can you imagine what Noah's friends thought as he went about constructing his barge? They had to have thought he was a few bricks short of a full load.

Noah's obedience cost him time, resources, pride, and even his reputation. But, the cost was worth it. Noah's obedience saved the human race from annihilation when God sent the Great Flood upon the earth. Noah was willing to count the cost of obedience because he was a child of God.

The Definition of Knowing God

Being willing to count the cost of obeying God is a sign that you are truly a child of God. 1 John 2:5-6 says, *"If anyone obeys his word, God's love is truly in him: Whoever claims to live in him must walk as Jesus did."* Intimacy with God is closely tied to obedience to God. *"Those who obey his commands live in him, and he in them."* (1 John 3:24)

Remember to count the cost of obedience to Christ. Budget this into your Extreme Spiritual Makeover plan. Become all that you were meant to be for eternity through obedience to God. You can do this!

Be Intentional

- Think about areas in your life where obedience to God is needed.

- Purpose to be obedient in your attitudes.

- Budget to endure any hardships that result with patience.

- Budget to be obedient to God, even if you look out of step with your culture.

- Budget to love other people, not judge them.

Questions for Personal Reflection or Group Study

- Has your spiritual transformation and obedience to God cost you anything? Please share.

- Do you find obedience to God hard or easy? Explain.

- How can your obedience end up benefitting others?

- Budgeting to be beautiful like God means counting the cost of obedience to Christ. Have you budgeted obedience into your spiritual makeover plan? Please share.

Day Twenty-two
Your Personal Makeover

A Jewel of Transformation: Obedience is a sign of true faith in God.

A Verse to Claim: *"If you really love me, you will obey my commandments."* (John 14:15)

A Question to Ponder: How can I make my life a picture of obedience?

Makeover Tip to Implement: Send a portion of your monthly budget to a ministry that sends Bibles to countries that need the Word of God. Be obedient to share the truth of God's Word with someone in your community.

Day 23
The Cost of Suffering

The little reed, bending to the force

Of the wind, soon stood upright again

When the storm had passed over.

~Aesop

There was an old violinmaker who would choose wood for his instruments from the north side of all trees on his property. The reason for this was that the northern part of the tree faced the fiercest windstorms. The trees would groan under the lashing of the violent winds and the trunk would bend under the force. This made the wood of the trees strong. It created a wood that made the most beautiful music. The storms taught the trees how to be violins.

The Certainty of Suffering

We all experience suffering. There is a body of false teaching in Christianity that says that if you have enough faith, you can avoid suffering and expect endless blessings from God. This is simply not what Christ taught. As a matter of fact, the Bible confirms that we can *expect* to suffer in I Peter 4:12, *"Do not be surprised at the painful trials you are suffering, as though something strange were happening to you. But rejoice that you participate in the suffering of Christ, so that you may be overjoyed when His glory is revealed."*

As part of your Extreme Spiritual Makeover, it is important to realize that suffering is part of your spiritual conditioning. Just as the story of the violin wood illustrates, it is often the hard things in our lives that produce the most beautiful character in our souls if we have the correct attitude about suffering. In the story, the storms come and the winds lash against the trees causing the tree trunks to bend, but not break. This is true of the trials in our lives, which can bring us to terrible lows, and force us to humbly bend to the will of God, rather than break in bitterness. The fierce winds that beat against the trees actually create a material that produces beautiful tones in the violin. God is a skillful craftsman using the trials and tribulations in our lives as tools to shape us, making us into beautiful instruments of praise and worship. But we must be willing to bend in our suffering and let the lashing shape our character. Do you realize that when you are lashed by the fierce winds of adversity, those difficulties can produce beauty in your soul that resonates peace, love, and joy to those around you?

Because Christ suffered on this earth and showed us how to face the certainty of trials with humility and faith, we can learn from him. Jesus encourages us when he says, *"I have told you these things, so that in me you may have peace. In this world, you will have trouble. But take heart! I have overcome the world."* (John 16:33) One way to have a proper attitude about the certainty of suffering is to realize that our suffering is intended to make us more like Jesus. Christ teaches in this passage that one of the keys to enduring suffering is to realize that Jesus has overcome this world. What does this mean? It means that Jesus will eventually make all things right on this earth. But it is so certain that he will do this that you can look upon it as already having been accomplished. You can bank on the fact that one day, *"He will wipe every tear from their eyes. There will be no more death or mourning or crying or pain, for the old order of things has passed away. Behold, I am making everything new!"* (Revelation 21:4-5)

Jesus does not teach that we are to figure out ways to *avoid* suffering. He wants us to have the proper attitude to get *through* our suffering. As we come to understand God's plan for humanity, we can pour hope into our cup of suffering. We can find peace in the fact that, one day, God will restore justice to the earth. Suffering does not just point us to the future when God will set things right, it also helps us live more fully in the present.

The Purposes of Suffering

The Principle of Pruning

If you ever decide to grow fruit trees, you will learn the importance of pruning. Steve Jobs, the founder of Apple, Inc., spent time as a young man in a commune that had an apple orchard. His responsibility as part of the commune was to prune the apple trees. The pruner is to examine the branches of each tree and cut off any branch that is not producing good fruit. On the good branches, the pruner is to clean off smaller twigs that will hinder fruit on the larger branch. The purpose of pruning is to stop the sap, which feeds the tree, from running into unproductive parts of the tree. When you cut off the bad branches, the good branches will produce more fruit because they will receive the sap that would otherwise go to the unproductive limbs. Steve Jobs relayed in later years that his work as a pruner taught him to simplify things and cut away unnecessary things that do not contribute to productivity. This principle helped him limit the number of products that Apple Inc. produced. Because of Steve Jobs' philosophy, the world has MacBooks, iPods, iPhones, iPads, and iTunes. The principle of pruning contributed to making Apple Inc. one of the most fruitful companies in modern times.

But this principle is not unique to Steve Jobs, Jesus first talked about pruning in John 15:1-2, *"I am the true Vine, and my Father is the gardener. He cuts off every branch that bears not fruit, while every branch that does bear fruit he prunes."* Jesus clarifies later in this illustration that his teachings act to prune or "clean" the believer. The Greek word for prune means purification or cleansing. Those things that are not fruitful in our lives will get cut away by the words of God in Scripture. *"For the word of God is living and active. Sharper than any two-edged sword, it penetrates even to dividing the soul and spirit, joints and marrow; it judges the thoughts and attitudes of the heart."* (Hebrews 4:12) This is one way that we are pruned, but there are other ways that God prunes us.

In order to protect us God will discipline us through the circumstances in our lives. Just as I may discipline my child by putting them in time out if they let go of my hand and run out into the street, or I may give them a swift tug, if they get too close to a hot stove, God can use suffering to prune us and take away those things that prevent us from abiding in Jesus, who is the true Vine. Whether our hardships are the natural consequence of being part of a world where sin is prevalent, or because of our own bad decisions, suffering can be a discipline that sets us back on the straight and narrow path of doing life by God's principles, rather than our own.

Suffering forces us to clarify our beliefs and reset our priorities. When someone is faced with the prospect of dying from cancer, they suddenly focus on what is truly important in life. Where they may have had work as their priority, after their illness, their faith and family become priorities. Suffering causes us to see what is preventing our own productivity and what might be hindering our spirituality, so that we can cut away the dead branches in our lives. This is how the principle of pruning works.

The Principle of Prosperity

Once God prunes us through suffering, we will reap the benefits of this cleansing process because God's Spirit inside of us acts as a holy sap that feeds our souls and produces the fruit of Godly character qualities in us. The Bible says, *"Not only so, but we also rejoice in our suffering, because we know that suffering produces perseverance; perseverance, character; and character, hope. And hope does not disappoint us, because God has poured out his love into our hearts by the Holy Spirit, whom he has given us."* (Romans 5:3-5)

When a plant is pruned back it often seems as though the plant will not survive the severe trimming. Pruning can leave a plant with almost nothing left. As the winter settles in, the prospect of the plant surviving looks grim. But as the warmth of spring rises, the plant will begin to bloom and grow. The pruning will have had its intended effect. Bursts of growth and fruit will come forth.

This is how we feel when God allows suffering to prune us. It hurts! It is often severe, and feels as though we will never recover, but the pruning results in the fruit of the Spirit bursting forth in our lives. **It is when we endure suffering**

that God brings love, joy, peace, patience, kindness, goodness, faithfulness, gentleness, and self-control into us to help us overcome our trials. As we persevere in troubles, our character, seen in the fruit of the Spirit, flourishes. As God produces these results in us, our lives are filled with the confidence that all of God's promises are true. *"For our light and momentary troubles are achieving for us an eternal glory that far outweighs them all."* (2 Corinthians 4:17) We then look forward to what Christ promised when he stated that he has overcome the world.

In addition to developing the qualities of Christ, we can embrace God's promise, *"All things work together for good for those who love God and are called according to His purpose."* (Romans 8:28) God's ultimate purpose for us as His children is to create faith, hope, and love in us. If we must suffer in order to become more eternally beautiful like Christ, than suffering will become a blessing. God promises that everything we go through is for a good purpose. Do you trust that this is true?

Becoming more eternally beautiful means counting the cost of suffering as a blessing.

Be Intentional

- Write a list of things you have suffered and what you learned from suffering.
- Purpose to release any bitterness you feel from past hardships.

- Purpose to think about your suffering as an opportunity to learn.
- Share what you have learned with one other person.

Questions for Personal Reflection or Group Study

- How is your life like the violin made from the wood that survived the storms?
- How can suffering make your character more beautiful?
- Explain the principle of pruning? What about the principle of prosperity?
- Share a lesson you have learned from your suffering.

Day Twenty-three
Your Personal Makeover

A Jewel of Transformation: Suffering is a tool God uses to enhance your eternal beauty.

A Verse to Claim: *"All things work together for good for those who love God and are called according to His purpose."* (Romans 8:28)

A Question to Ponder: How can I see my suffering as a jewel for eternity?

Makeover Tip to Implement: Write down a time that you suffered. Make a list of good things that came out of that trial. Thank God for the trial. Try this Bubble of Trouble Exercise: Take a bottle of bubbles. Blow out a bunch of bubbles and then pop as many as you can before they hit the floor. Think of each bubble as a past trial that is over and done. Let it go.

Day 24
The Cost of Faith

Commit your way to the Lord; trust in him and he will do this; he will make your righteousness shine like the dawn, the justice of your cause like the noon day sun.

~Psalm 37:5-6

We all need heroes. Whether it is an athlete who defies the normal boundaries of what is physically possible or a political leader who stands up for the rights of others, heroes inspire our faith and hope that one person can make a difference. Heroes are people of action. Perhaps, I should say these people are action heroes!

Being the mother of a boy, I know something about action heroes. Little boys are particularly drawn to them, and my son was no exception. By the age of three, his bedroom floor was littered with plastic Power Rangers, Ninja Turtles, and Star Wars characters. Batman, Spiderman, and even the Beast from *Beauty and the Beast* rounded out his collection. You would rarely see him around the house without an action figure in hand. Even at the kitchen table, his heroes waited patiently as he ate dinner. During this fabulous age of imagination, action heroes gave my son something to believe in. The ideals of helping people in need and saving the world from evil through courageous acts inspired my developing boy!

The neat thing about action heroes is that when faced with a problem, the hero has a definite set of beliefs that drives how they approach the problem. For example, Peter Parker (a.k.a. Spiderman) is inspired by his Uncle Ben's dying words, *"With great power comes great responsibility."* Peter believes in the truth of this statement and his faith in this philosophy guides him in everything he does as Spiderman. Because heroes have their faith so firmly rooted in certain principles, they are able to act with confidence in any situation.

As an Extreme Spiritual Makeover candidate, you, too, must be so rooted in your faith that you are able to handle life's challenges with the confidence that comes from knowing what you believe.

The Bible defines faith this way, *"Now faith is being sure of what we hope for and certain of what we do not see."* (Hebrews 11:1) This means that although we have not seen God, Christ, or eternity, we believe by our faith that what we hope for actually exists. This may seem crazy, but you and I act upon faith every day in many situations. For instance, every time you board an airplane you are acting upon faith. You are trusting that a metal tube with wings will be able to break the gravity of the earth, fly approximately 35,000 feet in the air at over 400 miles per hour, and get you safely to your destination. By boarding the plane, you act upon your faith and your reward for doing so is that you arrive at your destination.

Your spiritual faith works the same way. When you make decisions that affect your life based on the belief that there is a God and His promises are true, you have become a hero of the faith. Some of the promises that you must believe by faith are that salvation is possible through the death and resurrection of Jesus Christ, that God's Word in the Bible is true, and that there will be a new heaven and a new earth where you will live with God forever. Arriving at your heavenly home to live in God's presence forever will be the reward for your faith.

You can choose to be a hero of the faith by acting upon your faith in God each day. This kind of faith makes a difference for eternity. Fixing your eyes on the truth of things in eternity changes your perspective and the way you behave each day, here and now.

The Heroes of the Faith

In the eleventh chapter of the book of Hebrews, God gives us a list of heroes of the faith who did both large and small acts in reliance on what God told them, acting out of obedience based on their trust in what He said. This list of believers is often called "the hall of faith." These ancients obeyed, sometimes with small acts of obedience and sometimes with large leaps of faith. Be encouraged, as you study the lives of these faithful believers, that *you*, too, can respond to God's Word in obedience and be an action hero of the faith.

The book of Hebrews' hall of faith says that the ancient heroes of the faith lived out this principle, *"Now faith is being sure of what we hope for and certain of what we do not see. This is what the ancients were commended for."* (Hebrews 11:1-2)

The chapter goes on to list people who made intentional life choices based on faith. These people are God's action heroes who inspire us to live out our own faith. Let's look at some of the things that these action heroes of the faith accomplished that pleased God and won His commendation.

Adam and Eve are not mentioned in this hall of faith, but their son Abel is mentioned because when God demonstrated Jesus' future sacrificial death by killing some animals to provide clothing for Adam and Eve to cover their nakedness, Abel learned from God's example. Because of his faith, Abel gave an animal sacrifice to God as a sign that he believed God would provide a Savior in the future to cover the nakedness of his sins. Remember that in Genesis 3:15, God promised that a child would be born who would defeat Satan and conquer sin and evil in the world. Abel's sacrifice of an innocent animal mirrors Christ's future sacrificial death on the cross in the future. Abel's sacrifice was an act of faith in something that he could not yet see, but he nevertheless believed it would come to pass.

Another hero is Noah. We have already looked at passages about Noah's faith and obedience. He is mentioned here because he was warned about something he had not seen (the Great Flood), and he believed what God told him about the coming judgment on the earth. Because of this faith, Noah built the ark, saved his family, and condemned the unbelief of the rest of the people alive at the time who did not have faith in God's warning. Noah's actions confirmed his faith.

Abraham is considered by many to be the father of faith. God told Abraham to leave his homeland and travel to a promised land. Although he did not know his destination, he believed God when God said it existed and obeyed by moving there. The Scriptures tell us, *"For he was looking forward to the city with foundations, whose architect and builder is God."* (Hebrews 11:10) This passage clarifies that God saw Abraham's obedience as proof that Abraham also believed in the future eternal (new) heaven and earth (the final promised land) that God would build. Abraham could not see that place either, but by faith he believed that God would create a new heaven and earth for those who love Him. Abraham also believed God's promise that He would make Abraham the father of a large nation. You and I know that Jesus came from Abraham's lineage, but when Abraham had his son Isaac through Sarah, he was could not see into the future. It was his faith led him to impregnate his ninety-year old wife, trusting that God would fulfill His promise about bringing the Savior of the world to earth through his descendants. Abraham believed in what he could not see because of his faith that what God said was true.

This is the kind of faith that God wants from you, a faith that causes you to act upon the things that He promised to you, but that you have not yet seen. Hebrews 11:13-16 states,

> *All these people were still living by faith when they died. They did not receive the things promised; they only saw them and welcomed them from a distance. And they admitted that they were aliens and strangers on earth. People who say such things show that they are looking for a country of their own. If they had been thinking of the country they had left, they would have had opportunity to return. Instead, they were longing for a better country – a heavenly one. Therefore, God is not ashamed to be called their God, for he has prepared a city for them.*

The list of heroes continues with Isaac, Jacob, and Joseph. When we come to Moses' life, Moses was commended for identifying with the future Christ, rather than with the Egyptians who raised him in the Pharaoh's palace. He chose to identify with his people, the Hebrews, who were slaves in Egypt at this time. Chapter 11 explains that Moses did this because he believed in the coming Messiah. He trusted what God promised all those years ago in the Garden of Eden to Adam and Eve, that a child would come to save the world. That same faith led him to leave Egypt, keep the Passover, which was a picture of Christ's death seen in the slaying of an innocent lamb, and lead the nation of Israel through the parting of the Red Sea and back into the Promised Land. Moses obeyed God, not because he was immediately given what was promised, but because he had faith in what he could not see.

As you read Hebrews 11, there are many other heroes of the faith mentioned. Notice that the individuals highlighted did not always do something epic. More often than not, they simply approached the problem at hand through the lens of their faith. For some, their faith led to great personal suffering such as being tortured, flogged and killed. Others' faith led them to experience great triumph such as conquering kingdoms, shutting the mouths of lions, and even seeing their dead raised to life again. Once again we are told, *"These were all commended for their faith, yet none of them received what had been promised, since God had planned something better for us so that only together with us would they be made perfect"*. (Hebrews 11:39-40)

What is important is that these action heroes of faith believed what God promised and conducted their lives accordingly, as can you. They were looking forward to the birth of Christ, while you are looking back at his death and resurrection and forward to his Second Coming. So how can you become an action hero who will be commended by God when you see Him face to face?

Becoming an Action Hero of Faith

God is calling *you* to act in faith with whatever circumstances your life presents. God is watching and is pleased when your actions are guided by your faith in Him, your belief in His story, and your desire to follow His principles for living. Just as an action hero is guided by a set of principles, you life should be guided by Biblical principles. Your life will not look like your neighbor's life. The steps you take as you trust God will not mirror another person's. God made you uniquely individual and your individual life, if lived in faith, glorifies Him. His vast creativity demands billions of different faith hero stories in order to reflect His abundant mercy and love. As we take actions based on our faith, God weaves a beautiful tapestry of faith that will be displayed for eternity.

You can be an action hero of the faith. As a matter of fact, you were designed by God to be an action hero of the faith. Developing a beauty that will last forever includes acts of faith that make you more beautiful with each passing day.

Be Intentional

- Write out some promises of God found in Scripture.

- List decisions made in your life that were based on your faith in what God has promised.

- How has the truth that you will live forever with God changed how you approach your life today?

- Think about steps of faith you took that cost you a friendship or a relationship.

- List your gifts and talents. How can you use those natural abilities to show your faith in God?

Questions for Personal Reflection or Group Study

- Who are your personal heroes? Why are they your heroes?

- Explain why having life principles is important to a hero?

- Upon what principles are you basing your actions?

- Name a decision in your life that was made based on your faith in God and following Biblical principles.

Day Twenty-four
Your Personal Makeover

A Jewel of Transformation: Faith endures forever.

A Verse to Claim: *"Faith is the substance of things hoped for and the evidence of things not seen."* (Hebrews 11:1)

A Question to Ponder: How can I act today according to my faith?

Makeover Tip to Implement: Write down an act of faith that applies uniquely to your life experience. Do the thing that God is calling you to do.

Day 25
Becoming Like Christ

He must increase and I must decrease.

John 3:30

You were created for transformation. One of the keys to understanding God's story and how you fit into that story is to realize that it was always God's plan to redeem you, to reconcile the broken relationship between you and Him, and to transform you into His image. Adrian Rogers once said, "The same Jesus who turned water into wine can transform your home, your life, your family, and your future. He is still in the miracle-working business, and His business is the business of transformation." God does all of this at a tremendous cost because of His great love for you.

One reason the popular makeover shows are appealing to a wide audience is that the individual chosen for the makeover is usually unable to afford the procedures herself. The cost of the physical makeover, including surgery, dental work, nutritionist, fitness trainer, hair stylist, make-up artist, and fashion consultant, runs into the tens of thousands of dollars. Unless she is chosen for the makeover, the candidate has little hope of being able to make these changes on her own. Being chosen is the miracle. Once chosen, the candidate merely accepts the makeover. To see someone experience such amazing transformation as a free gift is heartwarming.

The same is true of you as an Extreme Spiritual Makeover candidate. You, too, are chosen. You have been chosen by God to be changed. God planned this for you even before you were born. This is your great miracle. The Bible says, *"Even before he made the world, God loved us and chose us in Christ to be holy and without fault in his eyes."* (Ephesians 1:4) (NLT) You, too, have been given a gift that you could not afford on your own. You must accept God's gift in order to experience the makeover. Your spiritual beauty comes at a tremendous cost. It was bought with Christ's blood, which was shed for *you*. His death makes your transformation possible. What a sacrifice! What a gift! God gives you the gift of salvation through Jesus Christ simply because of your faith in Him.

He also gives you His Holy Spirit to live inside of you, guaranteeing that you will live forever in a resurrected body with Him in a new heaven and a new earth. (Revelation 21 and 22) And, it is God's plan to choose you as an Extreme Spiritual Makeover candidate to transform you into the image of Jesus

Christ, even while you are on this earth in your present body. It is the Holy Spirit inside of you that begins to exfoliate your sinful tendencies, inspires you to eat the Bread of Life and drink the Living Water to live forever, and gives you energy to exercise your soul through love and good works. All of these things serve to change you to look more like Jesus. This is the essence of your Extreme Spiritual Makeover.

Transformation through Discipline

Although it doesn't cost any money, the recipient of the televised physical makeover must still count the non-monetary costs of undergoing the transformation, such as the pain of surgery, the separation from friends and family during the process, and the commitment to a new healthy diet and exercise regime.

The spiritual makeover candidate must also count the costs of becoming spiritually beautiful. Christ himself warned his disciples of the cost of following Him, *"If any of you wants to be my follower, you must turn from your selfish ways, take up your cross daily, and follow me."* (Luke 9:23) The cross was a symbol of death. What did Christ mean? Were his followers all to die on a cross? No. What Christ was referring to is the willingness of believers to *die* to themselves and *live* for God. This requires sacrifice.

This sacrifice may take the form of consistent Bible reading designed to help you know God, daily prayer for intimate communication with your Creator, humble reliance on the Holy Spirit for the power to be transformed, or acting upon your faith, even though your actions may result in hardship. Each of these disciplines will require your time, energy, and dedication. There must be passion and desire on your part in order to accomplish this. Jesus was passionate in his faith. It is how you, as his follower, must dedicate yourself to live. Your makeover will result in true and lasting beauty, as you become less like your sinful self and more like Christ.

Sacrifice means that you are going to surrender your will to God's will. The amazing thing about transformation is that when your mind becomes trained to think God's thoughts, your actions will begin to reflect God's acts more easily. Eventually, the sacrifice will feel less like pain and more like pleasure.

Transformation is a Process

You have spent your time wisely going through this Extreme Spiritual Makeover, but the lessons in this book are just the beginning of your transformation to eternal beauty. In order to fully reap the benefits of your makeover, remember to look into the mirror of God's Word each day to see how your soul looks. Exfoliate sin from your life. Be persistent and rub it out whenever you see it. Eat well by realizing that Jesus is the manna from heaven that sustains you forever. God's Word is your spiritual food.

Drink in the Holy Spirit. The Spirit is the fluid promise that will quench your soul's thirst for eternal life. As you drink in God's Spirit, it will comfort you, teach you, cleanse you, make you fruitful, and enable you to live forever. Make sure to walk in the sunshine of daily prayer with God. This is how you will get energy to face what life brings you and how you will shine forth to others. Keep doing cardio God's way with loving acts of kindness. Keep your spiritual muscles toned by carrying the burdens of others. Always remember that it is a marathon, not a sprint.

Get up each day and show the world that you are like Christ by dressing for success. Pick outfits from the believer's closet like justice, humility, kindness, strength, and righteousness. Wear an attitude of gratitude to God. Never forget to suit up for battle. Satan roams the earth seeking whom he might devour. Wear God's armor and prepare to stand against the schemes of the devil. Also, be sure to budget for beauty. Becoming like Christ will cost you. You will need to be obedient, endure suffering, and take action because of your faith.

Charles H. Spurgeon once said, "When we come to the end of self, we come to the beginning of Christ." Transformation is possible. The lowly caterpillar becomes the beautiful butterfly. The ugly duckling really is a beautiful swan. You really can and really will be transformed into the image of Christ, as long as you live by this principle, "He must increase and I must decrease!" This is true beauty that will last!

Questions for Personal Reflection or Group Study

- What did Jesus mean when he told his followers that they must take up their cross and follow him?

- What sacrifices are you willing to make for Jesus in your: 1) attitudes 2) actions 3) relationships 4) pride 5) expectations

- Discuss how you have changed over the last 25 days.

- Share one lesson that has transformed you.

- Share how this Extreme Spiritual Makeover has enhanced your beauty.

Day 25

Your Personal Makeover

A Jewel of Transformation: True beauty comes at a cost.

A Verse to Claim: *"We will all be changed."* (1 Corinthians 15:51)

A Question to Ponder: How can I decrease while Jesus increases in me?

Makeover Tip to Implement: Take a photocopy of the swan provided on the next page and put it on your mirror as a daily reminder that you are in the process of being transformed!

Weekly divisions for a thirteen-week study:

Week One
Introduction and Day 1

Week Two
Day 2 and Day 3

Week Three
Day 4 and Day 5

Week Four
Day 6 and Day 7

Week Five
Day 8 and Day 9

Week Six
Day 10 and Day 11

Week Seven
Day 12 and Day 13

Week Eight
Day 14 and Day 15

Week Nine
Day 16 and Day 17

Week Ten
Day 18 and Day 19

Week Eleven
Day 20 and Day 21

Week Twelve
Day 22 and 23

Week Thirteen
Day 24 and 25

Notes

Transformation Is Possible

1. Hans Christian Andersen, Translated by Erik Christian Haugaard, *A Treasury of Hans Christian Andersen* (New York, Barnes & Noble Books, 1974), The Ugly Duckling 167-175.
2. John Ortberg, *The Life You've Always Wanted* (Grand Rapids, MI, Zondervan, 1997), 21
3. 1 Timothy 3:16

Day 1: Am I Beautiful? Defining Beauty On God's Terms

1. Proverbs 31:30
2. Colossians 2:9
3. Philippians 4:8
4. Proverbs 23:7
5. Matthew 26:10,13
6. Proverbs 31:30

Day 2: You Were Created to be Beautiful

1. Witness Lee, *The Economy of God* (Living Streams Ministry, 1968, 1993), 70-71
2. Witness Lee, *Basic Lessons in Life* (Living Streams Ministry, 1993) Information on man being three parts
3. http://www.tripartiteman.org/definition/index.html copyright 2000, 2002 Information on man being three parts
4. 1 Thessalonians 5:23
5. Genesis 2:7
6. Zechariah 12:1
7. John 6:24
8. 1 Corinthians 15:51
9. Genesis 1:26-27
10. Genesis 1:26-27 (The Message)
11. Henry Bullinger- (1504-1575) Swiss reformer
12. Genesis 2:16
13. http://www.tripartiteman.org/salvation/index.html copyright 2000, 2002 Information on the effects of the fall on man
14. Ephesians 2:4-5
15. Romans 3:23
16. Romans 6:23
17. Romans 5:17

Day 3: Just One of the Family

1. Ephesians 1:4 (New Living Translation)
2. Ephesians 1:4-5 (Other Scriptures on being adopted into God's family include Romans 8:23 & Galatians 4:4)

3. Rick Warren, *The Purpose Driven Life* (Grand Rapids, MI, Zondervan, 2002) 117-121 The concept of being part of God's family
4. 2 Corinthians 5:17
5. John 3:3
6. John 3:16
7. Hebrews 2:10-13 (NLT)
8. Romans 10:9-10
9. Ephesians 1:14

Day 4: Say So
1. Psalm 107:2 (NLT)
2. Romans 4:3
3. Romans 4:22-25
4. Luke 3:21-22
5. Matthew 28:18-20
6. Acts 10:46
7. 2 Corinthians 5:17

Day 5: It's Time To Change
1. Anne Sandberg, *John Newton Author of Amazing Grace* (Uhrichville, OH, Barbour Books, 1996)
2. Genesis 32 Jacob's story
3. Hosea 12:3-5
4. Genesis 32:26
5. Revelation 19:7-8

Day 6: Into The Looking Glass
1. Hebrews 4:12
2. Exodus 20:1-17 The Ten Commandments
3. Matthew 5 The Beatitudes
4. Matthew 5:22
5. Matthew 19:26
6. James 1:25 (NLT)

Day 7: Embracing Self Examination
1. Jeremiah 17:9
2. 2 Chronicles 34 Story of Josiah
3. James 1:22-24
4. Galatians 5:16-21
5. James 1:22

Exfoliating Sin
1. Genesis 4:7
2. 1 John 1:9

Day 8: Rubbing Out Rubbish
1. Genesis 6-9 Flood story

Notes

2. Genesis 19 Sodom and Gomorrah story
3. Acts 5 Ananias and Sapphira incident
4. Psalm 32:2
5. John 8:5
6. John 8:7
7. John 8:10-11
8. 1 John 1:9

Day 9: Liposuctioning Excess

1. Acts 3:19
2. John 8:32
3. http://www.lwf.org/site/News2?abbr=for_&page=NewsArticle&id=9957&news_iv_ctrl=1261 Dr. Adrian Rogers, *The Purpose of Pain* Article, Love Worth Finding Ministries
4. Luke 22:42-44
5. Romans 8:31-33
6. Nancy Alcorn, *Echoes of Mercy* (Nashville, TN 1992, Revised 2002) www.mercyministries.com
7. Romans 8:37-39
8. Genesis 6:5-6
9. Genesis 7:1
10. Romans 8:28
11. Matthew 5:48 (The Message)

Food For The Spirit

1. Psalm 119:103

Day 10: Tasting Truth

1. John 6:23
2. Isaiah 49:15
3. Exodus 16 Manna in the desert
4. Deuteronomy 8:3
5. Matthew 4:1-4
6. John 6:32
7. John 6:51
8. John 6:35

Day 11: Fuel To Fight

1. John 4:22
2. J. Vernon McGee, Thru the Bible with J. Vernon McGee (Nashville, TN: Thomas Nelson, Inc., 1981) 23
3. Genesis 3:1-6
4. 1 John 2:16
5. Genesis 3:4-5

6. 2 Corinthians 12:9-10
7. Exodus 20:14
8. Deuteronomy 6:13
9. Exodus 20:17
10. Luke 4:8
11. Psalm 91:11-12
12. Job 13:15
13. James 1:17
14. Deuteronomy 6:16
15. James 4:7
16. Psalm 119:103

Water- Drinking In The Holy Spirit
1. Revelation 21:6

Day 12: A Fluid Promise
1. John 7:38
2. John 14:10
3. John 14:13-14
4. John 4:25
5. John 14:26
6. John 14:16-17
7. Ephesians 1:14
8. Galatians 5:25-26
9. 1 Corinthians 6:19

Day 13: Liquid Power
1. Luke 24:49
2. John 14:17-20
3. Acts 1:4
4. Acts 2
5. Acts 2:15-16
6. Acts 2:36
7. Joel 2
8. Galatians 5:22-23
9. John 15:5
10. Matthew 28:19-20
11. Romans 12
12. 1 Corinthians 12
13. Ephesians 4
14. 1 Peter 4:9-10
15. Romans 12:4-6
16. 1 Timothy 2:1-2
17. Exodus 28

Notes

18. Acts 9:39
19. Rick Warren, *The Purpose Driven Life* (Grand Rapids, MI, Zondervan, 2002) 236-237 Unwrapping your spiritual gifts.
20. Spiritual Gift descriptions taken from Storyline Bible Study- Windsor Crossing Church 2012
21. John 16:13

Day 14: Walking On Sunshine
1. Ephesians 6:18
2. Genesis 2
3. Daniel 9-12 Daniel's story
4. Daniel 9:4
5. Daniel 4:5-6
6. Daniel 4:15-16
7. Daniel 4:17-19
8. 1 Thessalonians 5:17
9. Matthew 6:9-13 King James Version
10. Luke 11:9
11. 1 Thessalonians 5:17

Day 15: Energy From Prayer
1. 1 Samuel 1:6
2. 1 Samuel 1:16
3. 1 Samuel 1:18
4. 1 Samuel 1:27
5. 1 Samuel 1:18
6. 1 Samuel 2:1
7. Luke 22:44
8. Matthew 26:38
9. Matthew 26:42
10. Matthew 26:50
11. Genesis 3:15
12. Revelation 20:10
13. Philippians 4:6

Day 16: Doing Cardio God's Way
1. Hebrews 10:24
2. James 2:26
3. Hebrews 13:16
4. Luke 10:27
5. Luke 10:36
6. Luke 10:37
7. Luke 23 Jesus' crucifixion

8. Luke 23:28-29
9. Luke 23:34
10. Luke 23:43
11. Luke 6:32-36
12. Matthew 19:26
13. 1 Thessalonians 5:14-15
14. Hebrews 10:24

Day 17: Carrying The Burdens Of Others
1. http://www.womenshealthmag.com/weight-loss/weight-training-tips Women's Health Magazine 2012
2. Galatians 6:2
3. Exodus 18:14, 17-23
4. Exodus 18:24
5. Luke 5:20
6. Galatians 6:2

Day 18: It's A Marathon
1. Hebrews 12:1
2. Hebrews 12:1-3
3. Hebrews 12:2-4
4. Revelation 21
5. James 1:2-4
6. 1 Corinthians 15:57-58

Day 19: The Believer's Closet
1. 1 Peter 3:3-4
2. Reference to Isaiah 64:6
3. Isaiah 61:10
4. Job 29:14-17
5. Proverbs 31:25-26
6. Luke 24:49
7. Colossians 3:12
8. 1 Peter 5:5
9. Romans 13:14

Day 20: An Attitude Of Gratitude
1. Psalm 100:4
2. Luke 17:12
3. Luke 17:15-16
4. Luke 17:17-18
5. Luke 18:39
6. Luke 18:42
7. Luke 18:43
8. 1 Thessalonians 5:8

Notes

Day 21: Dressed For Battle
1. Ephesians 6:10-11
2. Ephesians 6:12
3. Ephesians 6:13-17
4. Ephesians 6:10

Day 22: The Cost Of Obedience
1. http://www.news.com.au/money/money-matters/beauty-obsession-sending-women-broke/story-e6frfmd9-1111117238360#ixzz1zBftP043 The Cost of Beauty Article
2. Mark 16:15
3. Acts 6-8 Stephen is martyred
4. 1 Corinthians 1:18
5. Genesis 6:22
6. 1 John 2:5-6
7. 1 John 3:24
8. John 14:15

Day 23: The Cost Of Suffering
1. 1 Peter 4:12
2. John 16:33
3. Revelation 21:4-5
4. Isaacson, Walter *Steve Jobs* (New York, New York, Simon & Schuster 2011) 63
5. John 15:1-2
6. Hebrews 4:12
7. Romans 5:3-5
8. 2 Corinthians 4:17
9. Romans 8:28

Day 24: The Cost Of Faith
1. Psalm 37:5-6
2. Hebrews 11:1
3. Hebrews 11:6
4. Hebrews 11:7-27
5. Hebrews 11:27-35a
6. Hebrews 11:35a-38
7. Hebrews 11:38
8. Hebrews 11:1

Day 25: Becoming Like Christ
1. John 3:30
2. Ephesians 1:4
3. Revelation 21-22
4. Luke 9:23
5. 1 Corinthians 15:51

Made in the USA
Lexington, KY
04 August 2012